Bilingual in Chile: An Impossible Dream?

Thomas Jerome Baker

Revised, Reedited & Republished: November 2014

ISBN-10: 148019901X
ISBN-13: 978-1480199019

DEDICATION

This book is dedicated to all the teachers in Chile, and the entire world, who believe that English can be learned to a high level.

The most successful English learners begin from an early age, regardless of whether we are looking at Canada, Singapore, or Chile.

Yes, in Chile, we have bilingual students. They became bilingual without sacrificing the mother tongue, or the Chilean culture, or the heritage that identifies them as members of a particular linguistic community.

In the case of this book, I refer to the special nature of being Chilean, and speaking English. It is not a dream, bilingualism in Chile, it is reality, but only for a few.

"English for Everyone" is a task the teachers, parents, students, and nation of Chile must get serious about. We need to study our Chilean experience, and replicate our success in the private sector in the public sector.

This book, again, is dedicated to every teacher in the world who is involved in this noble endeavour. May God Bless You All.

CONTENTS

ACKNOWLEDGMENTS

All sources used have been acknowledged as fully as possible. For any omissions, I beg forgiveness in advance. Bilingualism, whether in Chile or in any other part of the globe, is a cause which merits attention from a wide range of people. When we can draw out its myths, and question them, then we can advance the cause of bilingualism on its merits, which is what it deserves.

I am thankful to all the individuals, named and otherwise mentioned, for the insights which have gone into the thinking behind this book. Again, I say most humbly, you are greatly appreciated.

CHAPTER 1

THE BILINGUAL ADVANTAGE

A cognitive neuroscientist, Ellen Bialystok has spent almost 40 years learning about how bilingualism sharpens the mind. Her good news: Among other benefits, the regular use of two languages appears to delay the onset of Alzheimer's disease symptoms. Dr. Bialystok, 63, a distinguished research professor of psychology at York University in Toronto, was awarded a $100,000 Killam Prize last year for her contributions to social science. http://research.baycrest.org/ebialystok

As you might imagine, her work has been very influential in helping educators the world over to understand bilingualism. Indeed, she has helped us to reach new perspectives about the advantages of bilingualism, and in particular, how the bilingual mind works.

For example, one of the most persistent myths about bilingualism is that it is not good for children to learn two languages at the same time. It is believed that it causes both languages, the mother language and the second language, to be incompletely learned, or less successfully learned than if the child had only been learning one language.

Dr. Bialystok recently published research that concluded with an endorsement of immersion education as a way to achieve bilingualism. The citation below is for the research which I am referring to. It shows English-speaking children in immersion education as early as 2nd grade able to enjoy lasting benefits from the immersion experience. It contradicts the popular belief that learning a foreign language, while a child, is harmful. This myth is not true.

Citation: Hermanto N., Moreno S. & Bialystok E. 2012. Linguistic and metalinguistic outcomes of intense immersion education: how bilingual? International Journal of Bilingual Education and Bilingualism, 15, 131-145.

Abstract

Anglophone children in Grades 2 and 5 who attended an intensive French immersion program were examined for linguistic and metalinguistic ability in English and French. Measures of linguistic proficiency (vocabulary and grammatical knowledge) were consistently higher in English and remained so even after 5 years of immersion education in French. Measures of metalinguistic ability (letter fluency and ignoring semantic anomalies in sentence judgments) in French improved significantly over the two grades studied and closed the gap (letter fluency) or caught up with (sentence judgments) similar performance in English. This dissociation between developmental trajectories for linguistic and metalinguistic development is exactly the pattern expected for fully bilingual children, endorsing immersion education as a route to bilingualism. **

Perhaps her most well-known research has to deal with the long term benefits of learning and using a second language. It has to do with delaying the onset of Alzheimer's disease in old age. The citation below is for that recent conclusive finding.

Citation: Craik F.I., Bialystok E. & Freedman M. 2010. Delaying the onset of Alzheimer disease: bilingualism as a form of cognitive reserve. *Neurology*, *75 (19)*, 1726-1729.

Abstract

...we conclude that lifelong bilingualism confers protection against the onset of AD. The effect does not appear to be attributable to such possible confounding factors as education, occupational status, or immigration. Bilingualism thus appears to contribute to cognitive reserve, which acts to compensate for the effects of accumulated neuropathology. **

In the third bit of research, Dr. Bialystok sheds light on how the bilingual mind functions during the lifetime, addressing both the benefits and the drawbacks of bilingualism. In brief, monolinguals generally have higher levels of language proficiency in a given language (drawback). On the other hand, bilinguals have ability to focus on the essential elements of a nonverbal task involving conflicting information. She calls this, "enhanced executive control".

Citation: Bialystok E. & Craik F.I.M. 2009. Cognitive and linguistic processing in the bilingual mind.*Current Directions in Psychological Science*, *19 (1)*, 19-23.

Abstract

The article reports research investigating the way bilingualism affects cognitive and linguistic performance across the life span. In general, bilingualism appears to have both benefits and costs. Regarding costs, bilinguals typically have lower formal language proficiency than monolinguals do; for example, they have smaller vocabularies and weaker access to lexical items. The benefits, however, are that bilinguals exhibit enhanced executive control in nonverbal tasks requiring conflict resolution, such as the Stroop and Simon tasks. **

She has an extensive body of work that is impressive in the sense that she has investigated the major topics that come up when one wishes to address the issue of bilingualism. According to her research, we can say that bilingualism has advantages. It acts as a sort of insurance policy in delaying or preventing Alzheimer's disease altogether. Immersion education for young children has benefits in promoting the development of bilingualism. Equally important, the bilingual mind is a sharper mind, enhancing the ability to process conflicting information in order to make rational decisions.

Dr. Bialystok's work is important because it establishes major benefits for bilingualism. In addition, there is motivation to consider. Bilingualism provides access to opportunity: social, economic, cultural. In particular, here in Chile we say, "English Opens Doors" of opportunity.

Consider the following excerpt from the New York Times, written on December 29, 2004, by Larry Rohter:
http://nyti.ms/UVboMZ

Learn English, Says Chile, Thinking Upwardly Global

"We have some of the most advanced commercial accords in the world, but that is not enough," Sergio Bitar, the minister of education, said in an interview here. "We know our lives are linked more than ever to an international presence, and if you can't speak English, you can't sell and you can't learn."

The initial phase of the 18-month-old program, officially known as "English Opens Doors," calls for all Chilean elementary and high school students to be able to pass a standardized listening and reading test a decade from now. But the more ambitious long-term goal is to make all 15 million of Chile's people fluent in English within a generation.

"It took the Swedes 40 years" to get to that point, said Mr. Bitar, adding that he sees the Nordic countries and Southeast Asian nations like Malaysia as models for Chile. "It's going to take us decades too, but we're on the right track." (end of excerpt)

As you can see, from this Chilean perspective, there is an instrumental motivation for becoming bilingual in English. It would mean economic prosperity. It would facilitate international business between Chile and other countries who do not share a common language. In sum, it would mean the ability to reap the benefits of an open, global economy.

So, why hasn't Chile become bilingual to the point necessary to promote its business interests? After all, it is now 10 years since the article above appeared in the New York Times. Is learning a language really something that can only be done in 40 to 50 years time? If the answer is "Yes", then surely the opportunities of the present day will be long gone before Chile is able to take advantage of its international free trade agreements.

A "Bilingual Chile", obviously requires patience. Bilingualism is coming very slowly for Chile. Bilingualism is still only a dream for most Chileans, and for many, an impossible dream. Considering our starting point, that sentiment is understandable.

In 2003, for example, a joint study done by the University of

Bilingual in Chile: An Impossible Dream?

Chile and the Ministry of Education found that only 4% of 15-year-olds self-evaluated as bilingual. In 2004, a diagnostic test was given to a sample of 11000 students from 299 schools in 8th grade and 12th grade. The pass rate was 5%. http://slidesha.re/QN6ehU In 2008 the pass rate was 10%. Progress was visible, yes, but agonizingly slow.

The first full test came in 2010, when over 208,000 students from 2600 schools, in 11th grade was tested. The pass rate, at level A2 on the Common European Framework of Reference (CEFR) was 11%. http://slidesha.re/Tt6uRu Again, progress yes, but slow.

Adults in Chile are just as bad as the students. In 2011, Education First (EF) released a three year study called the "English Proficiency Index" or EPI for short, that ranked Chile number 36. http://bit.ly/PYuujX Only one year later, Chile had fallen back to number 39 http://bit.ly/Tnqc4Z .

In the labor market, the study seems to be correlated. Trabajando.com cited the following figures: 80% of the professionals in Chile have a deficient level of English. http://bit.ly/SMGamG The Chilean government has promoted the learning of English by professionals by providing scholarships. In spite of this, it is estimated that only 2% of the population is able to use English at a level considered to be competent.

What explains the results reported above? According to Education First EF: "Spanish serves as an international language in Latin America. Therefore, Latin America's English proficiency is very low. In part this is explained by the importance of Spanish to the region. A shared language already allows for continental trade, diplomacy, and travel, lessening the motivation to learn English."

EF goes deeper into the matter and provides a more convincing explanation than merely pointing to Spanish as a shared language in Latin America. EF believes the poor quality of education in the region and the unequal access to education is the more likely cause of poor English proficiency. Most observers of education in Chile would likely agree with that analysis, but some further supporting evidence can be offered.

On the 2010 national standardised test of English, "Simce Inglés" , only 11% of students tested achieved a passing score. The top 100 schools included 97 private schools, with only 3 public schools. The top 16 schools all had perfect scores: 100%. This result suggests that EF is correct in assuming that socioeconomic status plays a significant role in the overall poor results in Latin America.

Although socioeconomic status is an intuitively attractive explanation for failure to learn English, there are researchers who have reached a different conclusion. For example, consider the following abstract:

Abstract

Using meta-analysis techniques, almost 200 studies that considered the relation between socioeconomic status (SES) and academic achievement (AA) were examined. Results indicate that as SES is typically defined and used, it is only weakly correlated with AA. (6 p ref) (PsycINFO Database Record (c) 2012 APA, all rights reserved)

Citation: White, Karl R. The relation between socioeconomic status and academic achievement. Psychological Bulletin, Vol 91(3), May 1982, 461-481.http://dx.doi.org/10.1037/0033-2909.91.3.461

To sum up, in this first chapter we have made the case that bilingualism is an advantage that opens the doors of economic opportunity. Unfortunately, there is no doubt that in Chile we are several decades away from becoming bilingual, judging by the current pace. In the next chapter, we will define bilingualism and then discuss what is holding Chile at a snail's pace in our efforts to become bilingual.

A final reflexion is in order before moving on. Is Chile, a bilingual country, nothing more than an impossible dream? No, as we have seen, it is not an impossible dream. It is simply going to take a very long time to get there. At our current rate of progress, increasing 1% every 2 years, it will take another 40 years to reach the 50% mark, and 80 years to make it to the 100% level, where the country is fully bilingual.

We have set off on a very long journey, indeed. Bilingualism, it seems, is a dream that is very much possible. However, we know we can not wait 80 years to become bilingual. That's too long.

CHAPTER 2

WHAT IS BILINGUALISM?

Bilingualism is easy to define, for me. I have no need to look in a dictionary on this one. Bilingualism is obviously the ability to speak two languages. Trilingualism would then be the ability to speak three languages. I find myself personally defined by both definitions.

I am both a bilingual and a trilingual, according to the definitions I have given. I became a bilingual in the spring of 1982, when I was 20 years old, in Neu Ulm, Germany. I still remember the day quite vividly. I had been studying German in the 40-hour basic German course that all new soldiers assigned to Germany were required to take after arriving in Germany.

Each day the teacher would build up our ability to say another phrase in German. It had begun with, "*Guten Morgen*". Then had followed, "*Ich heisse Thomas*". Next came, "*Ich bin aus Amerika*". And on and on it went every day, each day a new word, each day a new phrase. I was pleasantly surprised how easy German was. It seemed to be so much like English to me that I had no trouble understanding what our "*Lehrerin*, Frau Schmidt", wanted us to learn.

And to top things off, she liked going outside and having classes sitting in the shade of a tree. With the birds singing and spring in full bloom, the learning process for me was swift. So, here it was, Thursday, and there I was, speaking full sentences, communicating in German, for example:

"*Guten Tag. Ich heisse Thomas und komme aus Amerika. Ich bin Soldat von Beruf. Ich habe ein Bruder und 3 Schwestern. Ich möchte ein Bier bitte. Morgen gehe ich nach Hause.*"

Let me translate what I just said. It goes like this: (English translation follows) "Good morning. My name is Thomas, and I'm from America. I am a soldier. I have one brother and three sisters. I would like one beer please. Tomorrow I'm going home."

I couldn't believe I had said all that. I don't know where the beer came from but it looks like I was planning to follow up that beer with a few more because I wasn't planning on going home until the next day.

From that moment forward, **I was bilingual**. I could say things in German. I could introduce myself, tell you where I was from, what I did for a living, and talk about my family. I could ask for a beer and let you know when I was going home. Like I said, **I was bilingual.**

Now, that experience makes us take a closer look at **what it means to be bilingual**. I couldn't read German, couldn't write German, and didn't understand spoken German if it was spoken fast or used big words. Wait, I could handle the situation when you spoke too fast or used big words.

I would look at you, and say, quite seriously, "*Sprechen Sie langsam.*" Slow down. And when you slowed down, but still kept using those big words, I would say, "*Ich verstehe nichts.*" I don't understand a word you just said.

I was bilingual, wasn't I? Of course I was. Bilingual means you are using another language to communicate. Just like a baby crawls before walking, and says baby talk before talking, I was developing my ability to communicate. Just like a baby, I was a beginner. Only I was moving much faster than any baby had ever moved when learning to speak. In one week's time, I was introducing myself, talking about my family and my job, and ordering a beer to relax. Not to mention telling you when I would be going home.

Can you imagine a baby doing all that in a week? If something like that happened, with a real baby, in a week, I know I'd be amazed, and pretty scared too. Who knows what the baby is going to do next, drive a car?

Bilingualism then, is the ability to communicate. You understand spoken language first, then comes your speaking. Then comes reading and finally you get serious and start writing. This is what linguists call, language acquisition. Now, let's refer to some experts and see if my view of bilingualism will be acceptable or not. According to Carol Myers-Scotton, in her book, "***Multiple Voices: An introduction to bilingualism***" , there have been many attempts to define bilingualism from many different perspectives, but none of them works in general or really characterizes the phenomenon very well. For example, defining bilingualism as "speaking two or more languages with native-like ability" would rule out most bilingual speakers."

Hmmm. Is there anything more useful? She continues on page 44: "...bilinguals may show either **"active" or "passive" bilingualism**. That is, someone may be able to understand a certain L2, but not speak it, making him or her a passive bilingual."

That works out quite well with my version of bilingualism in German. Though I couldn't read or write German, I could speak it purposefully. Thus, I was an active bilingual. Is there anything else we need for a good working definition?

Myers-Scotton: "So, who is a bilingual? If we can't use proficiency in speaking another language as our criterion, what can we use? Most books and articles on bilingualism spend several sentences, if not several paragraphs, looking at one definition and then another. Surely knowing just a few words or phrases isn't enough to qualify a speaker as a bilingual. But how many phrases *is* enough? It depends on who is doing the defining. You can imagine that any definition that calls for being able to use two languages "perfectly" or even "habitually" won't work for us – given our discussion above. Even definitions that refer to "minimal proficiency" in a second language run into problems; for example, how is "minimal" to be defined?

For our purposes, we are satisfied with a very broad definition based on being able to **demonstrate minimal use of two or more languages**.

We have indicated that bilingualism may be based on reading or writing as well as speaking. But in this book we will consider **speaking** most **essential** in our definition.

We'll say that **bilingualism is the ability to use two or more languages sufficiently to carry on a limited casual conversation**, but we won't set specific limits on proficiency or how much the speaker in question is speaking or demonstrating comprehension of another speaker." (end of quote)

So there you have it. "**Bilingualism is the ability to use two or more languages sufficiently to carry on a limited casual conversation**." I was bilingual when I began to use it in a limited casual conversation.

Let's move on to our next concern in this chapter.

How can we explain the slow rate of progress of Chileans in becoming bilingual?

Immediately, we are able to see that the term, "bilingual" may actually already apply to Chileans. It is a matter of how you choose to define the term, "bilingual". In Chile, we seem to be applying **a proficiency standard** on our bilingualism.

When a certain number of people reach a certain proficiency level, then we will be bilingual. I can not help but think that the use of proficiency levels that have an international standard that is globally acceptable is a very good idea. When we say someone is "basic" level, everyone knows what the person "can do" linguistically.

Chile's Ministry of Education, English Opens Doors Program, set the standard at CEFR level A2, high Basic, as the goal for students to have achieved by the end of 8th grade. By the end of the 4th year in high school (12th grade) students are to have achieved CEFR level B1. Teachers are to have achieved CEFR level B2. http://bit.ly/S1ToMl

The Cambridge ESOL Main Suite of exams that correspond to the levels mentioned above are the Key English Test (KET) for level A2, the Preliminary English Test (PET) for level B1, and the First Certificate English (FCE) for level B2. http://bit.ly/WSZ5kM

With reference to the Cambridge ESOL Main Suite of exams it is important to note that the levels are not arbitrarily selected. The best source of information on this topic, the relationship between the CEFR and the Cambridge ESOL Main Suite of exams, can be found here: http://bit.ly/Rnyx7S . This is important to know because it gives a proficiency-based perspective on the issue of what a person Can Do with the language, based upon level of achievements that have gained universal acceptance as the gold standard in teaching and learning languages.

I quote Cambridge ESOL: "Cambridge ESOL was involved in the development of this standard (CEFR). Brian North, one of the authors of the Framework, has said that:

'We're really at the beginning of the process of validating the

claims which are made by the examination boards about the relationship of their exams to the Framework. There is a difference between having a very good idea of what the relationship is and confirming it. Cambridge ESOL is an exception, because there is a relationship between the levels in the CEF [Common European Framework] and the levels of the Cambridge ESOL exams.' (Interview with Dr. Brian North in *ELT News*, Feb 06.)

What else is interesting about the origins of the CEFR? Again, I turn to Dr. Brian North, one of the CEFR's authors, who confirms its **origins in traditional English Language Teaching levels**:

"The CEFR levels did not suddenly appear from nowhere. They have emerged in a gradual, collective recognition of what the late Peter Hargreaves (Cambridge ESOL) described during the 1991 Rüschlikon Symposium as "natural levels" in the sense of useful curriculum and examination levels. The process of defining these levels started in 1913 with the Cambridge Proficiency exam (CPE) that defines a practical mastery of the language as a non-native speaker. This level has become C2. Just before the last war, Cambridge introduced the First Certificate (FCE) – still widely seen as the first level of proficiency of interest for office work, now associated with B2. In the 1970s the Council of Europe defined a lower level called "The Threshold Level" (now B1), originally to specify what kind of language an immigrant or visitor needed to operate effectively in society. Threshold was quickly followed by "Waystage" (now A2), a staging point half way to Threshold. The first time all these concepts were described as a possible set of "Council of Europe levels" was in a presentation by David Wilkins (author of "The Functional Approach") at the 1977 Ludwighaven Symposium…(North 2006:8)." (end of quote)

When the majority of Chileans, both students and adults, reach the levels of achievement that have been set by the Ministry of Education, English Opens Doors Program, then we will consider ourselves to be, "**bilingual**", in a functional, proficiency-based sense, according to what we "Can Do" with the language.

Let's move on and try to answer the larger question: Why is our progress so slow in Chile? Immediately three factors come to mind: 1. Teachers. 2. Teachers. 3. Teachers.

What do I mean by blaming all teachers here in Chile (including myself) so indiscriminately?

Surely it's not our fault. We can't control things like poverty, hopelessness, helplessness, large classes of 40 to 45 students, frustrated and intrinsically unmotivated students, low pay, low levels of social prestige, lack of resources, lack of support, etc. This list could go on ad infinitum, without stopping for another page or so. Teachers control very few of the circumstances that impact on our performance as teachers.

So, let's be fair. For example, nobody would ever say something like: "It has been empirically proven that pilots have the most impact on flying a plane from one place to another". The statement is an oxymoron, **deafening** for the **silence** it produces. It's obviously, quite patently **true** because we recognize that without a pilot, the plane isn't going anywhere. Conversely, it's **false**, just as obvious and just as patently false that a pilot is going to fly a plane without the assistance of a huge team on the ground and in the air. Thus, we have the contradiction inherent in blaming teachers for lack of progress in learning English.

To be clear, flying a plane is a a team effort. Likewise, teaching a student to speak English is a team effort. The teacher is important, but without a team, neither the teacher nor the student is going to get very far.

So, let me rephrase. What we need, not only in Chile, but all around the world, is better teachers. I have three aspects in mind:

1. Highly trained teachers, with a requirement for C2 language proficiency in English. Teachers of English, who can't speak English, needs to be ended as soon as possible. For example, would anyone get on a plane with a pilot who could not fly the plane? Another example: Would anyone allow a doctor to operate on them, if the doctor did not know how to do the operation? Would anyone even get into a taxi if they knew that the taxi driver

could not drive? So, it is time to accept the fact that if a teacher can not speak English, they should not be allowed to speak English. Does that make sense, or is there something that I forgot to consider?

2. Pedagogy is essential. Just knowing a language does not enable you to teach a language. Studying how the students learn, and differentiating instruction so that all students learn is a moral imperative. The old paradigm of teaching, presenting material in one way (lecture) for all students, must give way to a multiplicity of strategies supported by educational theory.

3. Classroom management skills that create and sustain a favorable learning environment must be skillfully employed. Of the three aspects I mention, this one is equally important, but the least amenable to theoretical precepts. It is in the practice where successsful classroom management skills are acquired. If I am pressed for three points I consider crucial for classroom management to be successful, I would name three "Be Statements": 1. Be fair, 2. Be predictable. 3. Be human.

To sum up, I am advocating for teachers who can teach English, in English (thereby bringing the language alive). These teachers also need to know educational theory, and apply it eclectically, to help all students to be successful, each according to their needs. Finally, in regards to classroom management, a good starting point for teachers is to be fair, predictable and human. Within that triangle, most human interactions in a classroom will play out. The exceptions a teacher will encounter present themselves as opportunities for further growth and development.

Next, let's address the other issues that keep teachers and students from being successful. More than anything else, socioeconomic status seems to be the greatest factor in determining whether or not a student will learn English in Chile. 97 out of the 100 best schools on the Simce Inglés 2010 test came from private schools. So, what can a teacher do about that issue, poverty?

First, let me give an example. In Austria, teachers of English are supposed to reach level C2, the highest level of proficiency on the CEFR. That corresponds to the Cambridge Proficiency Exam level on the Cambridge ESOL Suites exams. In Chile, by contrast, future teachers of English are recommended to reach level B2, which corresponds to the First Certificate Exam level. Compared to

Austria, our standards for newly trained teachers are too low, in terms of what level of English we expect from teachers. Our expectations and demands on the training of new teachers are too low.

However, Chile does have highly trained, highly competent, bilingual teachers. How do I know this? When I look into the employment pages of the newspaper today, the most popular paper, "El Mercurio" is prominently displaying ads by private schools who are looking for bilingual teachers. There is no doubt in my mind that the ads will result in bilingual applicants being found, and subsequently hired. Private schools have bilingual teachers because they pay a higher salary for that level of expertise, the ability to teach your subject in English.

The lesson we take away is a simple one. Teaching Mathematics in English, Science, History, teaching any subject in English, is a skill that is currently available in Chile. Why not require all teachers to have this ability, and then increase the salary of the teachers who achieve this level of ability: being a bilingual teacher? Right now, it's a privilege that is only for those who can afford it.

A second point is directly tied to the first point. We have found that teachers who teach English in English have better results than teachers who teach English, in Spanish. However, if a teacher has not mastered the language while at university, is it logical to expect that the teacher ever will have the self-motivation to continue improving their English to a high level? Of course not.

It has been pointed out that we don't have enough teachers of English in the country. Many students have teachers who are not qualified teachers of English. Put another way, there are not enough trained teachers in the country. A notorious shortage exists. What can be done about this teaching shortage? How do you achieve quantity, and quality, in the teaching profession.?

Firstly, let's look at what has been done so far. The government has taken on the task of upgrading the language proficiency skills of practicing teachers. Year after year, beginning in 2003, courses on English language and methodology have been offered. Scholarships to study higher levels have been awarded. Language courses, methodology courses, semester study abroad in English-speaking countries, workshops, immersion training, teacher networks, native speaker teaching assistants, debates, spelling bees, summer and winter programs for students, etc. have been facilitated by the English Opens Doors Program. A tremendous amount of energy and resources have been used to improve the current practicing teachers and to produce better qualified new teachers. All this has been in effect for the past 10 years. Yet it still isn't enough. We have to do more.

Doing more means maintaining all of the current programs and initiatives. Everything that is being done is adding on to the eventual momentum that is needed to reach a higher performing teaching force. Teachers at all levels can do their part by having the willingness to share, to collaborate, to cooperate, with their colleagues.

Day by day, we get closer and closer to the ultimate goal we all strive for. We are striving for bilingualism that adds value, bilingualism that creates opportunities for the country to prosper, as well as for all of its citizens. Just how important is bilingualism for Chile? Consider the recent findings of Education First (EF) about the impact of English: "English is the primary tool for international communication today. In a world where global integration is the norm, such a tool is necessary for larger portions of the population in more diverse situations than ever before."

• English is a key component of economic wellbeing, both nationally and individually. Better English proficiency goes hand in hand with higher incomes, more exports, an easier environment for doing business, and more innovation.

• English skills flourish at the crossroads. Those who do business abroad, work in multinational environments, or use the internet already speak English.

• Careful planning, correctly aligned goals, and adequate investment are necessary to teach English to a high level in schools.

• Women speak English better than men worldwide and in almost every country.

• Young professionals, aged 25-35, speak the best English of any group. They need English to get along in a modern workplace. Students exiting secondary school often do not have sufficient English to function effectively in such a working environment.

• Industries that work globally, like tourism and consulting, are the best at English. Nationally focused industries employ those with weaker English skills.

• Europe's English is the best of any region, but some European countries need to get serious about teaching English to a high level if they are to keep up with their neighbors.

• Despite having some of the best-performing school systems in the world, Asian countries are not educating their children to a high level in English. Countries where English is an official language have only slightly higher proficiency than others in the region.

• The Middle East, North Africa, and Central and South America have uniformly poor levels of English, despite reasonable levels of spending on education.

• Immigration to an English-speaking country is no guarantee of attaining English fluency. The level of general education and English skills prior to immigration, as well as access to education after arrival, seem to be key mitigating factors" (EF English Proficiency Index, pg. 3, 2012). http://bit.ly/Tnqc4Z

By now, there is no doubt that becoming bilingual in English, at a high level, will benefit everyone. In the next chapter, we will look at the instruments that have to come together if we are to succeed rapidly in this endeavour.

In conclusion, we did two things in this chapter. We defined "bilingualism" in a manner that stresses attaining a proficiency goal established by the Mineduc. Just knowing a few words and phrases isn't good enough. Secondly, we looked at how the learning of English is important. Perhaps Thomas Keller said it best when he was asked about what bilingualism is. Keller, a trilingual, said that bilingualism was a habit that had become a way of life. To achieve the beneficial effect of the habit, it needed to be practiced on a daily basis. I find myself in agreement with him. The full interview can be read on pages 2 and 3, here: http://bit.ly/MU57hg

Finally, to achieve the benefits that come with bilingualism, we need to find more creative ways to improve the teaching and learning of English in Chile. In the next chapter, we take a look at another context (international business), to see if we can draw inspiration from it to use in our context in Chile.

CHAPTER 3

"RAKUTEN" MEANS BUSINESS

Rakuten – A Japanese Company that Requires Its Japanese Employees to speak English – with each other!

Rakuten
楽®天
Shopping

Source: Daisuke Wakabayashi http://bit.ly/U7BfMa

When Rakuten Inc. introduced an **English-only policy for company communications in May 2010** as part of founder and CEO Hiroshi Mikitani's push to globalize the Japanese Web commerce firm, critics questioned the wisdom in forcing staff to communicate with each other **in their non-native tongue**, English. Two years later, Mr. Mikitani said the "**Englishnization**" policy has been a success with **steady improvement** in the English proficiency of Rakuten's staff and a greater willingness to communicate in comprehendible, if not perfect, English. As of April, Rakuten said 79% of documents, meetings and internal communications are conducted in English, an increase from 65% a year earlier.

The company is now taking the next step. Rakuten employees are required to use English in all internal presentations, documents and memos. In addition, all internal meetings, training sessions, and internal company emails will use English.

"It is not just preferable, it is really critical for us to be able to do business and operate in English," Mr. Mikitani said at the Foreign Correspondents Club of Japan. "Our staff doesn't need translators."

Mr. Mikitani, a former banker turned billionaire Internet entrepreneur, said one of the things holding back Japanese firms from competing globally is a language barrier that prevents them from fully grasping overseas competition. He also said the lack of English proficiency limits Japan Inc. from pursuing global talent and retaining non-Japanese staff.

According to research conducted by private education company EF Education First, Japan ranks 14th globally with "moderate proficiency" in the global English Proficiency Index behind South Korea and ahead of Portugal. The rating seems low, considering the amount of classroom hours devoted to teaching English in Japanese schools.

After implementing the policy, Mr. Mikitani said the company hadn't offered much support, hoping that people would learn on their own. But sensing that this change was causing a great deal of stress and anxiety for the staff, Rakuten decided to provide **free English classes**, offered **time to study**, and made clear that **learning English was a part of their job**.

Mr. Mikitani said some staff resigned unwilling to go along with the new policy, although he said the number is fewer than most people would think. He said the staff doesn't need to become native speakers. They just need the courage to try.

"It's not easy. It wasn't easy for me and it wasn't easy for my employees," said Mr. Mikitani. "I'm hoping that this is the beginning of this trend for Japanese industries, corporate Japan and the society in general."

Test scores indicate that the hard work is paying off. The average score on the Test of English for International Communication by Rakuten employees improved 32% from October 2010 to this June.

Watch Hiroshi Mikitani, CEO of Rakuten, discuss the company's English-only policy: http://bit.ly/1tUlhv2

**

The above story illustrates the point that Thomas Keller was making about bilingualism. When you make bilingualism a way of life. As a way of life, it becomes transformative. It transforms the possibilities for social, economic, and personal success. Doors that were previously closed are suddenly open.

In this sense, the Rakuten story is definitely worth studying closely. What would happen if you asked your Chilean employees to communicate with each other in English? How many employees would you lose? Rakuten, in the example above, lost some employees.

Surely they felt it was absurd for Japanese coworkers to communicate with each other in English, rather than in Japanese, the mother language. And of course, traditional employers in Japan, in the automotive industry for example, laughed at Rakuten.

Rakuten has weathered the storm, and they are now reaping the benefits of their company language policy. Test scores have risen, some by as much as 32%. This result can be explained by the "time on task" principle. The more you practice English, the better you get.

The same principle is at work in Chilean schools. Students whose teachers teach the whole class in English have better results than students whos teachers teach the class in Spanish. It is not hard to understand the reason why. The one student has greater long term exposure to the language. The Rakuten example follows this principal, increased time on task.

What else can we learn from the Rakuten example? The question of support is an issue. At first, Rakuten offered no support, hoping the employees would learn on their own. Rakuten soon discovered that simply mandating the use of English would not be enough to achieve the desired result.

Therefore Rakuten provided free English classes, provided time to study, and made it clear that learning English was considered to be a part of their job. This level of emphasis and support clearly combined to produce much better results for their employees. A positive benefit was the reduction of stress and anxiety related to the policy.

How might such a policy look like in the Chilean context? First, I think we should look at the government. What is the government doing to support the teaching and learning of English? The last three presidents of Chile, Sebastián Piñera, Michelle Bachelet, and

Ricardo Lagos, all three could speak English. They made speeches and gave presentations in English. There are numerous videos on the internet which give testimony to their abilities.

Second, what about for employment? In the newly formed Agency of Educational Quality, a job advertisement appears today. It states that an intermediate level of English is highly desirable. So, although English is not required for the position, it suggests that two evenly qualified candidates would ultimately use the English language proficiency to determine which one would get the job. It's a step in the right direction, there is no doubt about that. It sends a clear signal that learning the English language is a valuable activity for a professional. They call it "value added".

What about the private sector in Chile? Are there any examples to share of how companies promote the learning of English? Let's take a look at the Chilean branch of the company Price Waterhouse Cooper. The company was interviewed in 2010 for the Spanish version of the ETS magazine, "Innovations". In the Spring 2012 issue, the English version appears. Here are some choice excerpts from that article:

Workplace English: One Company's Example

English-language proficiency is highly prized in the global economy. To maximize the value they bring to their global clients, the Chile offices of global consulting company PricewaterhouseCoopers (PwC) operate an English language training program.

Carlos Lenck, Director of Human Capital, discusses the company's experience in Chile.

Innovations: *Why is English-language proficiency so important in Spanish-speaking Chile?*

Carlos Lenck: We live in a globalized world in which information, business and commerce constantly flow across national borders. That is very true for PwC in Chile. We serve business owners, executives and technicians whose colleagues at global headquarters and around the world communicate in English.

Many of our clients are audited in English and have English-speaking representatives here. Many of the reports they send to their headquarters must be in English. PwC, therefore, must provide services in English.

When a person joins our organization in Chile, he or she will actually be working for two companies: a small one serving Latin America and Spanish-speaking countries, and a global enterprise with 170,000 employees.

Our employees are members of a borderless business universe in which English is a common language. English-language proficiency also allows our employees to take advantage of the benefits offered by a company whose official language is English.

Q: What incentives do you provide employees to learn English?

C.L.: We offer English-language learning programs the day an employee starts on the job. We pay for 60 percent of the cost of English-language studies in a voluntary program available to all employees.

We do not offer 100 percent financing because we believe the value that someone assigns to an activity is higher when he or she has a personal financial commitment.

And English-language proficiency is a skill that people want to have.

Q: Do employees who speak English earn more than those who don't?

C.L.: Yes. Everyone who joins PwC takes an English-language proficiency test, which marks the beginning of their language study. They continue in the study program as long as necessary to accomplish the goals they set for themselves.

When someone scores 750 or above on the *TOEIC®* test, he or she will earn an "English bonus," which for an assistant translates into 25 percent of his or her salary, and for a supervisor or manager equals 20 percent of salary.

Q: *What is the "immersion abroad" program?*

C.L.: The "icing on the cake" is the incentive to study and learn English abroad. Employees with good performance records can undertake a six-month program in an English-speaking country.

They earn their salaries during that period and we finance 50 percent of the travel costs and course fees. For the first four months, the employee lives with a local, English-speaking family close to the university or institute where their courses are conducted.

For the last two months, they live on campus and are expected to be self-sufficient, as any student would be. They also participate in weekend trips to experience the other language and immerse themselves in the culture.

Q: *What other advantages for an employee are associated with English competency?*

C.L.: We recognize the bilingual difference and value professionals and administrative staff with bilingual skills. The latter, for example, could get a 40 percent salary differential for being able to communicate in English.

At PwC, you do need English-language skills, among others skills, for career advancement.

Q: *Are you apprehensive about training people who may later leave the company?*

C.L.: Experience shows that people who have worked here leave with a positive attitude about PwC. That person becomes a potential client.

This article was translated and adapted from the December 2010 issue of ETS Innovations *en Español. Available at http://bit.ly/T95Lsv*

Bilingual in Chile: An Impossible Dream?

**

We have now seen two companies who have taken contrasting English language proficiency policies. The contrast lies in the fact that in the one company, "Rakuten", employees are required to use English with one another, in Japan. On the other hand, the Chilean office of PricewaterhouseCoopers (PwC) has tied English language proficiency to financial incentives.

Based on what we have read, there is little doubt that both companies can claim success. In the case of PwC, when one looks at the vast amount of material published in English, to include articles, interviews, publications, and stories, their success is visibly on display. This is not the case with Rakuten. Yet we are aware that at Rakuten the entire company is involved with English, from the very bottom of the organization to the very top, the CEO himself.

Rakuten has been thorough. Their business involves E-commerce, much in the way that Amazon and Ebay have modeled it for those of us who are familiar with their business approach. E-commerce means everyone is Rakutan potentially is in contact with people from all over the world, 24 hours a day, 7 days a week. To accomplish that major feat, they had to amplify their ability to successfully communicate with the entire world.

In a CNN interview, Rakuten's owner and CEO, Hiroshi Mikitani, was asked why English was so vital for Rakutan. He responded: "If you want to be able to share expertise and knowledge, across an organization, everybody needs to be able to communicate in English. We're doing global business." http://bit.ly/SQgmpF Evidently, Rakuten has started a trend in Japan of making English proficiency a part of everyday business culture within the organization. Other firms have followed the lead of Rakuten. When your annual transaction volume is reported to be 8 billion pounds, it is probably a good idea to follow the lead of Rakuten's English language policy.

The same argument, facilitating global business, might also be made by PwC. They are also involved in global business. Their company website is an obvious example: it is available for reading in English or in Spanish. Here's how PwC describes their business:

Ethics and Business Conduct

PricewaterhouseCoopers ("PwC") is one of the world's pre-eminent professional services organisations. As professional advisers we help our clients solve complex business problems and aim to enhance their ability to build value, manage risk and improve performance. As business advisors we play a significant role in the operation of the world's capital markets. We take pride in the fact that our services add value by helping to improve transparency, trust and consistency of business processes. In order to succeed, we must grow and develop, both as individuals and as a business. Our core values of **Excellence**, **Teamwork** and **Leadership** help us to achieve this growth.

While we conduct our business (PDF - 775Kb) within the framework of applicable professional standards, laws, regulations and internal policies, we also acknowledge that these standards, laws, regulations and policies do not govern all types of behaviour.

As a result, we also have a Code of Conduct for all PwC people and firms. This Code is based on our values and it takes them to the next level - demonstrating our values in action. The Code also provides a frame of reference for PwC firms to establish more specific supplements to address territorial issues. Read more about PwC here: http://pwc.to/SlnfSz

In conclusion, this chapter was about the reality of English proficiency. In terms of global competitiveness, English is currently the best way to communicate with the world. Learning English, whether in the Rakuten model, a transformative bilingual experiential model, or in the PwC model, rewarding successful efforts with financial bonuses, is not the issue. We have seen the issue is really about making the commitment to achieve success. Both Rakuten and PricewaterhouseCoopers are committed to their employees having high levels of proficiency in the English language. Undoubtedly, a similar commitment on the part of people in Chile would provide access to greater opportunities for everyone.

In the next chapter, we want to pivot and take a look at two initiatives aimed at increasing the English language proficiency of teachers. The experience of Vietnam and Russia should provide some useful insights.

CHAPTER 4

RUSSIAN MINISTRY OF EDUCATION & THE REPUBLIC OF TATARSTAN CHOOSE EDUCATION FIRST (EF)

From the left: EF English First's CLLS Russia Country Manager, Mr. Edward Baldakov; CLLS President Cristoph Wilfert; Mr. Thomas Bertelman, Ambassador of Sweden; Mr. Albert Gilmutdinov, Minister of Education in the Republic of Tatarstan and Ms. Irina Romanets, Deputy Mayor of the City of Sochi, in Moscow, 20 October 2011.

EF Education First (EF), the world leader in international education, today signed an agreement with the Russian Ministry of Education and Science of the Republic of Tatarstan. EF Education First is to start a large-scale language education program covering more than 3,000 current and future English teachers, heads of Ministries and agencies of the Republic of Tatarstan, as well as volunteers and all the Republic's school children and students.

The official signing ceremony took place in EF's new central office in Moscow, with the participation of the Minister of Education and Science of the Republic of Tatarstan Albert

Gilmutdinov and Edward Baldakov, Country Manager Russia, EF Corporate Language Learning Solutions. The signing and opening ceremony of EF's new office was also attended by, amongst others, Vitaly Mutko, the Minister of Sport, Tourism and Youth Policy of the Russian Federation; Anatoly Pakhomov, Mayor of the City of Sochi; Dmitry Chernyshenko, President of Sochi 2014 Organizational Committee and H.E. Tomas Bertelman, Ambassador Extraordinary and Plenipotentiary of the Kingdom of Sweden to the Russian Federation.

EF's large-scale education project is supported by the President of Tatarstan Rustam Minnikhanov. During the first stage of the project EF will start training all the Tatarstan English teachers with the help of the largest online English language school in the world, EF Englishtown.

Today Tatarstan's developed IT infrastructure allows innovative projects to be implemented across its education system: all teachers have personal laptops and all the schools and universities will be provided with wireless Internet access. 3,409 teachers will take a special one-year course, 'EF Englishtown for professional teachers'; the innovative online school will allow the results and progress of each program participant to be tracked.

Based on the results of the online training, the 300 teachers with the best records will be sent to the international EF language centers in Great Britain and the USA to take an advanced training course and obtain one of the world's most prestigious certificates, the Cambridge Teacher Knowledge Test.

They will form a pool of highly qualified teachers in the Republic of Tatarstan, with the highest possible level of English proficiency attested by international educational organizations.

The heads of Ministries and agencies of the Republic of Tatarstan will also study English with EF within the framework of the project. The overarching goal of the cooperation between EF and Tatarstan is the creation of a favorable base level of information in order to increase people's interest in learning English.

That is why EF is providing a one month free trial of access to the EF Englishtown online school to every student in Tatarstan, which amounts to about 273,000 people. EF will hold an English language competition for all the Republic's schoolchildren.

Following the English teachers, it is planned that the teachers of other subjects will also start learning with EF.

Albert Gilmutdinov, Minister of Education and Science of the Republic of Tatarstan:

> "Tatarstan considers developing English a priority. Our republic invests significant amounts into developing education and information technology, and that's why we have chosen EF Education First – the recognized leader in online education – to implement the education program. EF's innovative solutions and the talent of our teachers will soon allow Tatarstan to make a great leap forward in its knowledge of English, which will substantially increase our population's competitiveness in the local, regional, national and world markets."

Christoph Wilfert, President of EF Corporate Language Learning Solutions: "We are proud that our company was chosen by the Republic of Tatarstan to implement such a large-scale education program. EF offers the region a multi-layered strategic approach to improving people's command of English. EF Education First is continuing to develop quickly in Russia. We are sure that Tatarstan's cutting-edge experience will be a model for other regions of Russia."

EF Education First is actively increasing its presence in Tatarstan. EF plans to open an office and several schools in the Republic. Moreover, EF is proposing that its experience of preparing for large sport competitions, such as the Olympic Games in Seoul in 1988 and Olympic Games in Beijing in 2008, be used to teach English to volunteers and personnel of the Student Games in Kazan in 2013.

About EF Education First

The international company EF, founded in 1965 with the mission "to break down barriers of language, culture, and geography", is the world's leading education company. EF has helped more than 15 million students to learn new languages and travel abroad. EF Corporate Language Learning Solutions specializes in teaching languages to corporate and private clients, in studies abroad, cultural exchange programs and in obtaining international certificates and has served more than 1,200 companies. EF is the official provider of the XXII Olympic Winter Games and XI Paralympic Winter Games 2014 in the City of Sochi in the "Foreign Language Teaching" category. EF is also teaching 80,000 persons in Brazil in preparation for the World Football Championships in 2014. More information is available at

EF Colaboraciones y Patrocinios.

The results of the EF English Proficiency Index, an innovative piece of research and the first index to display the practical English skills among the adult populations of different countries, are published at www.ef.com/epi.

For more detailed information please contact: press@ef.com

**

$450 Million Dollar Plan: Vietnam demands its Non-Native English Teachers have Intermediate English Level

All school leavers will have a minimum level of English by 2020 under ambitious education reforms, but teachers fear that they are not getting the help they need to upgrade their own skills.

Ed Parks
http://bit.ly/QODK7p

More than 80,000 English language teachers in Vietnam's state schools are expected to be confident, intermediate-level users of English, and to pass a test to prove it, as part of an ambitious initiative by the ministry of education to ensure that all young people leaving school by 2020 have a good grasp of the language.

As part of the strategy, which includes teaching maths in English, officials have adopted the Common European Framework of Reference (CEFR) to measure language competency. Teachers will need to achieve level B2 in English with school leavers expected to reach B1, a level below.

But the initiative is worrying many teachers, who are uncertain about their future if they fail to achieve grades in tests such as Ielts and Toefl.

"All teachers in primary school feel very nervous," said Nguyen Thi La, 29, an English teacher at Kim Dong Primary School in Hanoi.

"It's difficult for teachers to pass this exam, especially those in rural provinces. B2 is a high score."

"All we know is that if we pass we are OK. If we don't we can still continue teaching, then take another test, then if we fail that, we don't know."

Despite reports in state media, the education ministry maintains that no one will be sacked who does not achieve B2, equivalent to scores of between 5.0 and 6.0 in the IELTS test, in the countrywide screening.

"It's a proficiency test to identify how many teachers need government-funded language training before they can go on teacher training courses," said Nguyen Ngoc Hung, executive manager of Vietnam's National Foreign Languages 2020 Project.

"No teachers will be sacked if they are not qualified because we already know most of them are not qualified. No teachers will be left behind and the government will take care of them. But if the teachers don't want to improve, then parents will reject them because only qualified teachers will be able to run new training programmes."

Project 2020 will affect 200 million students and 85% of the $450m budget will be spent on teacher training, according to the education ministry.

Officials say proficiency equivalent to B2 is necessary so that English teachers can read academic papers, which will contribute to their professional development.

The state media recently reported that in the Mekong Delta's Ben Tre province, of 700 teachers who had been tested, only 61 reached the required score. In Hue, in central Vietnam, one in five scored B2 or higher when 500 primary and secondary teachers were screened with tests tailored by the British Council.

In the capital, Hanoi, teachers are taking the IELTS test and

18% have so far made the B2 grade. The education ministry said that in one province, which could not be identified, the pass rate is as low as one in 700.

So far testing has been voluntary. Candidates are required to provide certificates from test aligned to the CEFR, such as IELTS, Cambridge Esol exams and TOEFL.

Some trainers think that the B2 level need not be an obstacle for many teachers, but they say pay incentives are needed if the government is to retain teachers and find 24,000 more to meet its 2020 education targets.

"B2 is achievable enough. The teachers I know want to improve their English but want their salaries to be higher so that they can have an incentive to try harder to meet the standard," said Tran Thi Qua, a teacher trainer from the education department in Hue.

Education ministry officials say they are working to increase primary English teacher salaries. Some parents of primary-aged children are prepared to give their children's English teachers extra money.

"My biggest worry is where and how my children will learn English. There is a huge demand for English teaching at state primary schools. I have to spend lots of time and money now to give my children an English language education," said Do Thi Loan, a mother of two from Hanoi.

"The government needs to fund courses to help improve the quality of the teachers, and pay them more money, but I think if teachers don't want to improve, then they should change jobs," she said.

A new languages-focused curriculum delivered by retrained teachers should be in place in 70% of grade-three classes by 2015, according to ministry plans, and available nationwide by 2019. English teaching hours are set to double and maths will be taught in a foreign language in 30% of high schools in major cities by 2015.

But according to one language development specialist, the education ministry's goals are unrealistic.

Rebecca Hales, a former senior ELT development manager at British Council Vietnam, said: "The ministry is taking a phased approach, which is commendable, but there are issues with supply and demand. They don't have the trained primary English teachers.

The targets are completely unachievable at the moment."

According to Hales the British Council has been instrumental in the training 2,000 master trainers, but she doubts that local education authorities are willing to put money into spreading those skills further.

"The teacher trainers we trained up are now at the mercy of the individual education departments. There's no evidence at this stage of a large-scale teacher training plan," Hales said.

Nguyen Ngoc Hung asserts that a training strategy is in place, but acknowledges the scale of the project.

"I have invested in universities and colleges from different regions, sent their teachers to the UK and Australia, and turned them into teacher development centres that will reach out to train people in remote provinces," Nguyen said.

"There are many challenges. We are dealing with everything, from training, salaries and policy, to promotion, how to train [teachers] then keep them in the system. I'm not sure if [Project 2020] will be successful. Other countries have spent billions on English language teaching in the private sector but still governments have been very unhappy with the outcomes."

**

Ed Parks is a pseudonym for a journalist working in Vietnam
**

Commentary:

These two reports from different corners of the world, Russia and Vietnam, show one common thread. The teachers who are teaching the English language have to be competent in the language. It is a safe bet to say that learning a language, from a teacher who can not speak the language they are teaching, is like getting on a plane with a pilot who can not fly the plane. In both cases, the final destination will not be reached successfully.

Another common thread we see in the two reports is the issue of costs. The large scale of the effort in both cases means a tremendous financial investment. It is not a one time investment either. For the program to prosper over a long period of time, the financial resources will have to be sustained beyond the lifetime of the people who are currently making the decisions.

Thus, we see the inherent necessity to separate language policy from the realm of contested politics. If this is not done, any advances made could easily be lost when a change occurs in government.

Therefore, successful language programs that lead to bilingualism require concensus building. The concensus has to be shared with everyone, transparently, and then reinforced continuously. A failure to do so dooms the most promising efforts to ultimate underperformance, if not direct failure. Thus, we should examine the two initiatives (Russia and Vietnam) for evidence of such a national concensus. First, the plans from Vietnam are showing government leadership, Ministry of Education and Training, but a concensus is not visible.

The plans for teachers form part of MoET's National Foreign Languages 2020 Project. Manager of the project, Nguyen Ngoc Hung, said, "For years, we have put an over-emphasis on whether English teachers have **the right diploma or certificate**, not on their **actual listening, speaking, reading, and writing skills**."

It seems that Vietnam is not the only country in the world that is discovering that its teachers of English can't teach English, in English, and therefore have been getting by in the classroom by turning English into a grammar based subject. Again and again, the world over, the lament is heard: "After 7 to 10 years of learning English, and all you can say is, "**This is a pencil**".

I wish I were joking, but President Rafael Correa of Ecuador made that statement about learning English in Ecuador. Evidently the sad state of affairs caused him to embrace the most rigorous education program in the world, the International Baccalaureate Diploma program, with its high standards and universal acceptance by employers and universities alike, for the future of his country. He enrolled 125 public schools into the prestigious program in 2012.

In Ecuador, it was discovered that only 2% of the teachers of English in that country could speak English. President Correa called it a "social fraud" that had been tolerated for generations. Hence the move to bring in the rigor of the IB Diploma program, because the phrase, "this is a pencil" will not be tolerated as evidence of learning English.

In Colombia, things are not much better. According to a report by Andres Sanchez of Colombia's Central Bank, 93% of high school graduates speak no English, 5% speak basic English, 2% have an intermediate level and just 1% have advanced.

The report also said that one of the main causes of the poor standard of English among Colombian students is the lack of teachers in this subject area.

Caracol Radio reported that the president of Padres de Familia parents association, Carlos Ballesteros, blamed universities for not adequately preparing teachers of English and said that the curriculum should be revised to better prepare future teachers.

As we all know, this year the Chilean Ministry of Education is testing the proficiency level of teachers of English. Further, access to certification exams is provided for those teachers who have the likelihood of actually passing the exams that certify their level of English. It will surprise no one, however, if the number of Chilean teachers who actually achieve certification is not very high. By the end of the year, the actual figures will be known. It is forseeable that a level of C1 will actually become the required level that a teacher leaving university must certify before being allowed to teach. I do not doubt that anybody would vigorously oppose such a measure.

Turning to the Russian initiative with Education First (EF), it looks to be the most promising option at the moment. The scale is low, and their experience with the Beijing Olympics is definitely admirable. That is to say, they have a track record of success. That is a very important consideration. Again, EF has the "KnowHow" and the technology to succeed where others are failing miserably.

From the standpoint of concensus building, EF has the participation of the entire population. There can be little reason to doubt that the hopes of a nation have been mobilised behind this effort at becoming bilingual, leveraging the power of technology. Will a high level of enthusiasm, energy and motivation be enough to ensure success? I answer, quite carefully, "Maybe".

It will take EF a long way, this wave of positivity in their endeavour. Yet I do believe, EF will have to work long and hard, with a short term contingency plan and a long term, train the trainer, who trains the trainer, who trains the trainer, cyclical program. That said, I would like to be in the favorable position they are in. With a bit of hard work, and a little luck, their outlook is the best I've seen in a long time for a national bilingual project to succeed: http://bit.ly/1u9z9BG

"As Russia continues to delight and surprise in its transformation, EF English First is part of this change. With over 35 English language schools across the country and new schools opening all the time, EF is experiencing rapid expansion in this region. By teaching with EF, you will be part of this development. English language teaching in Russia is your ticket to see this incredible country first-hand."

**

EF takes the next step in partnership with Republic of Tatarstan's Ministry of Education

LONDON, Feb. 5, 2014

EF Education First, the world leader in language training for business, government and the education sector, announced today the signing of a Letter of Acceptance with Republic of Tatarstan's

Ministry of Education, taking their partnership into its second phase for another four years.

The first phase of the partnership was the co-development of "Ana Tele", an online school based on EF's cloud-based platform for studying Tatar. The project aims to preserve the Tatar culture and its language which, in addition to Russian, is the official language of the Republic. Ana Tele has taught 10,000 students during its first year. The second phase involves over 40,000 students, taught by teachers provided by the Ministry, while EF provides support and maintenance of the Ana Tele school.

The Ministry's investments in language training were also recently expanded to include English training via EF's online school -- training more than 5,000 teachers, students, professors, and public sector employees.

Peter Burman, President of EF Corporate Language Learning Solutions, commented: "We are extremely proud to be the long term partner of the Republic of Tatarstan in these prestigious projects." Mr Burman continues: "We are unique in that we can easily scale our resources to address the entire population of 4 million citizens with an affordable cloud-based school featuring live teacher classes."

Fattakovh Engel Navapovich, Minister of Education and Science of the Republic said, "Education is a key priority for the Republic of Tatarstan. EF's online learning platform has allowed us to reinforce use of the Tatar language, which is integral to our heritage and culture, while also focusing on the future by learning English. We are very proud of Ana Tele and results from this partnership and look forward to continued success over the next four years."

EF already partners with various government entities to help thousands of teachers, students and public sector employees in language training, including the Saudi Ministry of Education (T4EDU) and the Saudi Electronic University, The French Ministries of Defense and Interior. EF is also the Official Language Training supplier to the Olympic Winter Games in Sochi in 2014 to 70,000 participants of the Sochi 2014 Organizing Committee.

The strategic partnership with the Republic of Tatarstan's Government is an important step for EF in its future expansion in

Russia. It demonstrates the capability to develop and provide solutions for all the various needs in the country.

About EF Corporate Language Learning Solutions

EF Corporate Language Learning Solutions, an EF Education First company, is the world leader in corporate language training for multinational businesses and public sector organizations. Thousands of organizations and millions of students worldwide have put their trust in us for a reason - we have proven time and again that our training solutions generate real results. With a worldwide network of offices in over 50 countries, executive language institutes in Cambridge, UK and Boston, USA and the world's most advanced online, on-demand language school, EF CLLS, provides the highest returns on language training investments. For more information on EF Corporate Language Learning Solutions please visit:

http://www.ef.com/corporate (http://www.ef.com/loc).

About The Ministry of Education and Science of the Republic of Tatarstan
http://mon.tatarstan.ru/eng

For further information please contact:

Susan Nilsson
Director of Communications
susan.nilsson@ef.com (mailto:susan.nilsson@ef.com)
Tel: +44-74-3269-2538

**

In conclusion, this chapter gave us a sobering look at the current reality of two high profile bilingual projects. Both can be successful, but if I were placing any bets, I'd make my bet on EF in Russia. It looks like a winner, in every sense of the word. Next, we take a look at Canada, a country where bilingualism has long been a winner.

CHAPTER 5

ONE COUNTRY, DEUX LANGUES

Canada has long been a country in which two languages, English and French, live side by side, as unilingual majorities. This close proximity resulted in Canada recognizing English and French as the official languages of the country in 1968, in the "*Official Languages Act*". The act also created the position of "Official Languages Commissioner", who is an ombudsman, or monitor, on how the law is being carried out. That post is filled today by Dr. Graham Fraser, who makes an annual report about issues related to the Official Languages Act as part of his responsibilities.

While one may be led to think the act created institutional bilingualism, it is misleading. The intent of the law was to ensure the rights of Canadian citizens to be able to get government service in the language of their choice.

For example, In Quebec, 95% of the people speak French. If you don't speak French, what can you do when dealing with the government? Of course you speak English, because the law guarantees you that the government must provide someone who speaks English to serve you.

According to the 2011 census, Quebec was the only province to increase its rate of bilingualism in English and French since the last census in 2006. This comes as little surprise, because of its high saturation with people who speak French (Francophones).

Overall, the national rate of bilingualism in English and French rose from 17.4 to 17.5 per cent of the population from 2006 to 2011, according to the census. This is equivalent to an increase of 350,000 people, for a total of 5.8 million Canadians out of a total population of 33.1 million.

But the increase was largely driven by Quebec, where 42.6 per cent of the population said they had knowledge of both English and French in 2011, up from 40.6 per cent in 2006. Statistics Canada estimated that Quebec was responsible for 90 per cent of the increase across the country. http://bit.ly/VVNeU2

30000 children are in French immersion classes and 1,4 million doing "core French". http://bit.ly/Vxzw3Q

The Office of the Commissioner of Official Languages is responsible for protecting language rights and promoting English and French in Canadian society. Reporting directly to Parliament, the Office of the Commissioner has a mandate to ensure that federal institutions comply with the *Official Languages Act*. Graham Fraser is the current Commissioner.

**

FOR IMMEDIATE RELEASE

Canadians need greater access to second-language learning, says Graham Fraser

Ottawa, October 16, 2012: In the lead-up to Canada's 150th birthday, Commissioner of Official Languages Graham Fraser is recommending that the Prime Minister double the number of young Canadians who participate each year in second-language exchanges across the country in order to promote a better understanding and appreciation of Canada's linguistic duality.

"Despite the fact that the *Official Languages Act* is now into its fifth decade, it is still a challenge for some to recognize linguistic duality as a Canadian value and as a key element in Canada's identity," says Fraser. "It is important that the government do a better job of stressing the importance of Canada's official languages and increasing the opportunities for second-language learning by working with post-secondary institutions, the provinces and the territories."

The Commissioner's recommendation is included in his 2011–2012 annual report. The report stresses that, in five years, when Canadians celebrate their country's 150th anniversary, they should be able to celebrate Canada's linguistic duality—and enjoy its presence—across the country.

"Ultimately, the future of Canada's linguistic duality depends on two factors," explains Commissioner Fraser. "The degree to which English-speaking Quebecers and French-speaking Canadians outside Quebec are able to maintain a strong, vital linguistic environment in which they can live their lives fully in their language, and the degree to which Canada's two majority communities embrace Canada's linguistic duality as a key element in Canadian identity, regardless of whether they speak both official languages."

The annual report also includes an analysis of a typical visitor's experience in the National Capital Region, a study announced last year amid considerable interest. The objective was to determine whether it was possible to be served in French at various locations throughout Ottawa and in English in Gatineau.

"Our observations showed that there is substantial bilingual capacity for visitors to Canada's capital, but that it is often invisible," says Fraser. "Almost all hotel employees we met in downtown Ottawa could serve their guests in both languages, but greeted visitors only in English in almost all cases.

"In a way, bilingualism is Ottawa's best-kept secret."

The Commissioner's report also includes several examples of Canadian companies that are more competitive because they operate in both English and French.

In Canada, as elsewhere, clients generally prefer to do business in their first official language and feel more comfortable when they use it.

According to Commissioner Fraser, "the federal government does not hesitate to support Canadian businesses when they need to acquire new skills that give them a competitive edge in the market. It should therefore support them in their efforts to leverage and promote linguistic duality in Canada and throughout the world. This will create a win-win situation for the Canadian economy and for consumers."

As in previous years, the annual report describes investigations, audits and court remedies that were used to take a closer look at how a number of federal institutions complied with the*Official Languages Act*. It also reports on the number of complaints filed by members of the public and employees of the federal public service, which is an indication of compliance issues within federal institutions.

The complete report and recommendations are available on the Office of the Commissioner of Official Languages' Web site. Follow us on Twitter and Facebook.

**

Well, that was an interesting overview of Canadian language duality. Bilingualism in Canada is an entirely different matter than bilingualism in Chile. It is definitely, to cite Thomas Keller, "a way of life".

Yet I can not help but come away with the feeling that bilingualism in Canada is about maintaining your cultural identity, your heritage, by living in the monolingual community of your choice. A further point of interest is marriage. Will the partner speak both languages and raise the children as bilinguals, or will the spose be unilingual? Interesting indeed.

Beyond your individual cultural identity, I sense the effort to maintain a sense of national unity by embracing the other through his or her language of choice. We feel part of a shared community, a sense of belonging. We all like it when someone else speaks your language. You feel like you belong, and not like an outsider. It makes things comfortable, especially when one is seeking some service.

As you can see, this is a matter that is quite complicated, and resists my attempts at a speculative analysis. I am content to recognize that the Chilean definition of bilingualism could never suffice for the Canadian manifestation of bilingualism. The Chilean view of bilingualism is instrumental, while the Canadian identity is cultural and identity-driven, therefore defining both an individual's choice of membership in a group, community or nation.

**

FOR IMMEDIATE RELEASE

Target 2017: Graham Fraser calls for leadership to ensure equality of English and French in celebrations

Gatineau, October 7, 2014: Commissioner of Official Languages Graham Fraser is urging federal institutions to ensure that official languages are fully represented in the federal celebrations for the 150th anniversary of Confederation in 2017.

"In the national events leading up to 2017, English and French need to be seen and heard on equal footing. It's a time to celebrate our Canadian history and remember that our common thread is the relationship between English-speakers and French-speakers," said Mr. Fraser. "The time to plan is now."

Preparing for 2017 is the object of one of two recommendations included in his 2013–2014 annual report to Parliament. In the report Mr. Fraser also offers a close look at his activities aimed at helping protect language rights, including complaint investigations, audits, institutional 'report cards' and court interventions.

Mr. Fraser says common problems among federal institutions are inadequate planning and lack of consideration for official language minority communities.

In his analysis of the complaints he received related to the Deficit Reduction Action Plan, the Commissioner found that organizations still make decisions without considering the impact on official languages communities or on service delivery in both official languages.

"Success is no accident," said Mr. Fraser. "It's entirely possible for federal institutions to meet budget requirements while respecting the*Official Languages Act*. To be successful, institutions need to plan carefully, consult official languages communities that may be affected, and monitor progress on an ongoing basis. Failures arise when institutions neglect planning. And planning requires leadership."

The annual report also includes several concrete examples of how complaints filed by Canadians led to positive outcomes for all Canadians."When I receive a complaint and investigate it, it's an opportunity for a federal institution to turn a situation around and make a lasting change," said Mr. Fraser.

As in previous years, Mr. Fraser also found that institutions are struggling with greeting Canadians in both official languages in person. He therefore included a second recommendation in his report that also speaks to the importance of fully valuing Canada's two official languages.

He calls on the Canada School of Public Service and the Treasury Board Secretariat to examine and improve training on official languages for managers, new recruits and human resources professionals in the federal public service.

"To make real progress in serving Canadians and in respecting federal employees' rights, we need training for public servants to have a stronger emphasis on the importance of official languages," said Mr. Fraser.

**

I now pivot to take a look at French immersion education in Canada. To begin, if you speak English (Anglophone), then French will be your second language. We can call this FSL for short.

Core (basic) French	Extended French	Intensive French	French Immersion
French is the object of instruction. It is taught as a subject for about 20 to 40 minutes each day. This is by far the most common FSL program in the country.	Type of core French program in which additional exposure to French is provided. For example, French will be the language of instruction for an additional subject such as social studies.	Relatively new core French program where half of the school year is dedicated to intensive French instruction (up to 75% of the day spent on learning French), and the other half is spent on the regular (compacted) curriculum.	French is the language of instruction for a large portion of the subjects taught in class, as opposed to being the object of instruction.

French-immersion education in Canada

When French is not a language used in the home, formal instruction in school is often the most convenient option for children to learn it. French immersion is one of several French as a second language (FSL) program options available in elementary and secondary schools across Canada (see text box). Canada saw the opening of its first French-immersion class in 1965, in St-Lambert, Quebec.

Since then, French immersion has become available in all provinces and two territories. Most programs were developed following parental dissatisfaction with the traditional core French programs and the desire to encourage bilingualism among their children.

There are several types of immersion programs that differ along two dimensions: age of first French instruction and intensity of French instruction.

Early immersion begins right at the start of schooling in kindergarten or grade 1, while delayed immersion does not begin until the middle years of elementary school, and late immersion after that. An important difference between early and delayed or late-immersion programs is that training in second-language literacy precedes training in first-language literacy in early immersion.

In total French immersion, all classes are taught in French, usually for the first three years of the program. English-language arts classes are introduced in the fourth grade, followed by a gradual increase in English instruction for other subjects. In partial French-immersion programs, a varying proportion of classes (usually 50%) are taught in French. This proportion typically remains stable throughout the program.

Does French immersion work?

Research conducted in Canada during the past 40 years has shown that French immersion students outperform English students in regular core French programs in all types of French-language tests. Immersion students, especially those in early immersion, have been found to perform as well as native French students on tests of reading and listening comprehension. However, French-immersion students do not typically show native-like proficiency in speaking and writing skills, although their linguistic deficiencies are generally not a serious obstacle to their effective use of French for academic or interpersonal purposes.

The level of French proficiency attained by immersion students depends on the age of first instruction and on the extent of French instruction. Total-immersion students tend to outperform partial-immersion students on all types of tests.

Early-immersion students show higher degrees of proficiency in reading, listening comprehension, oral production, grammar and writing than late-immersion students.

Early-immersion students also tend to outperform delayed (or middle) immersion students on some French tests, though the differences in performance are sometimes small.

English-language skills

Since immersion programs focus on curricular instruction in French, a natural concern, especially with early total-French immersion, is that students' native language development may suffer. Typically, students in total early immersion receive no instruction in English until the third or fourth grade when English language arts are introduced for the first time.

During the first years of their immersion programs, early total-immersion students tend to score lower than students in English school on English-language testing of literacy skills (such as reading comprehension, spelling and written vocabulary).

However, most studies indicate that they show improvement in these skills after the first year of English-language arts instruction (introduced in grade 3 or 4).

In a recent Ontario study, early-immersion students in grade 3 and grade 6 were found to perform as well as their English-school counterparts on English reading and writing skills. In addition, a recent report based on data from the Programme for International Student Assessment (PISA) suggests that 15-year-old French-immersion students perform better on reading-assessment tests than non-immersion English students, even when tested in English.

Academic skills

In French-immersion programs, the same academic content is taught as in the regular English program. Since the language of instruction in French-immersion programs is the students' second language, it is important to determine whether these students perform as well as students in non-immersion programs who are being taught in their first language. Generally, research indicates that French immersion students perform as well, and in some cases better than English students on tests of science and mathematics.

A recent study compared the mathematics achievement of students enrolled in different kinds of French-immersion programs in Vancouver. In the regular immersion program, mathematics classes were taught in French up to grade 3, after which they were taught in English. In the new immersion program, mathematics classes continued to be taught in French in grades 4 through 7.

Results indicate that students who continued learning mathematics in French performed better on mathematics tests (administered in English) than those who were taught in English after grade 3.

*

It is important to note that factors other than French-immersion education likely play a role in these differences. These factors include self-selection, parental-educational attainment, and greater availability of immersion programs in more affluent and urban communities where literacy tends to be higher.

Adequate supply of qualified French-immersion teachers

There is a shortage of qualified French-immersion teachers in most provinces. In areas where demand for French-immersion services is growing, this shortage means that many districts are unable to provide spaces for all children who wish to enrol in French-immersion programs. For example, in British Columbia some school districts have implemented lottery systems because parents were lining up overnight to get their children enrolled in immersion programs. The teacher shortage is particularly acute at the secondary level, where teachers are required to have content area expertise in addition to their French-language skills.

Long-term solutions to this issue will require expanded opportunities for postsecondary learning in French, as well as opportunities and incentives for teachers to develop their French-language skills during their teacher preparation. In the short term, innovative approaches will be required. For example, video conferencing is being introduced in Alberta so that teachers with specialized knowledge can deliver classes to other schools through remote connections. http://bit.ly/S72Mh6

**

It is time to bring this chapter on Canada to a close. It has been informative and exciting to look at a country in which intuitively one expects a much higher rate of bilingualism. At 17.5% of the total population, the number is lower than I had expected to find.

I am impressed by the various programs for French immersion language teaching. Each one has its pros and cons. I identify the teaching of English in Chile as belonging to the core language program. As the intensity and amount of French the student is exposed to increases, the program changes its character.

The most important question is teaching immersion French to children at a very young age. Almost intuitively, one expects the student to suffer tremendous setbacks in the native, non-instructed language. Yet, according to the evidence presented, this does not occur. I now turn to look at bilingual education in Chile.

**

CHAPTER 6

The Chilean Way: Four Models of Full Immersion English

How does English immersion look in the Chilean private schools? Let's take a peek at some instructional models. Keep in mind that each of the models come from actual Chilean schools that are highly successful. From this lens, we can ask ourselves to what extent all or parts of the model might be successfully adopted in the public schools.

Model 1:

(the common approach for bilingual English-Spanish education in Chile)

"Our committment with respect to the acquisition of English enables our pupils to become bilingual or highly proficient in the English language by the time they graduate. The entire learning process takes place **through the English language when our pupils are at a young age** – this is what we understand as **full immersion from Play Group to Year 6**. From Year Seven onwards, the teaching of English is comprised of a rich and varied programme of studies reinforced by the school environment itself."

**

Model 2:

(the "British-influenced" approach to for bilingual English-Spanish education in Chile)

"The Senior School curriculum is a blend of national and international programmes that aims to prepare our pupils for further studies at the university of their choice anywhere in the world. The international curriculum is linked to the Cambridge

IGCSE and A Level programmes and all pupils are prepared for international examinations in a wide array of subjects in 2nd and 4th Medio.

The School also teaches the Chilean National Curriculum in preparation for the PSU, Chiles university admissions examination. Both programmes are taught in an integrated approach throughout the School. In the Senior School all pupils must study English as a separate subject and many other subjects use English textbooks and resources.

Pupils are required to study Sciences, Mathematics and Social Studies. They are expected to communicate to a very high standard in Spanish and English both orally and in writing). IGCSE and A Level are all in English. Our pupils at The Grange are usually fluent in both languages by the time they leave School."

For more information please visit the Cambridge International Exams Website : **www.cie.org.uk**

**

Model 3: (an extensive look at a school designed to cater to the international community. Dual influence: British and American)

A school called, "The International Preparatory School" or **TIPS** http://tipschile.com/

Founded in 1975, The International Preparatory School is a small, international school located on beautiful grounds in the foothills of the Andes in Santiago, Chile. The International Preparatory School provides a distinguished education for children from 2 to 18 years old, beginning in Playgroup and continuing to Year 13 (Grade 12). With its British-based curriculum, nurturing atmosphere and dedicated staff, The International Preparatory School offers the individual care and attention that allow children of all ages and abilities to thrive. The school is committed to fostering a secure happy, and stimulating environment in which students are inspired to reach their full potential by developing a lifelong love of learning.

Bilingual in Chile: An Impossible Dream?

The International Preparatory School offers the international community the opportunity to place their children in a local school while ensuring that they receive a multicultural education of the highest international standards. Our small class size and favourable student/teacher ratio facilitate this personalized approach. Each child develops his or her academic ability and a strong sense of identity, well-being and self confidence.

The International Preparatory School also provides an alternative for parents from the national community who would like their children to develop strong English skills and multicultural awareness to better prepare them for the challenges of an increasingly complex world. Our students make lasting connections with children from diverse backgrounds and cultures and world cultures. They cultivate a strong language foundation and acquire flexible skill sets as they prepare to become global citizens.

Playgroup

As playgroup is often a child's first experience in a school setting, the children are encouraged to adapt to their new learning situation and to integrate into the group. Playgroup children develop their language skills through a variety of activities. They are encouraged to share their experiences with their classmates and teachers and to express their ideas using simple and then more complex sentences. The children gradually develop their listening skills and expand their attention spans.

The Foundation Stage

The Foundation Stage is a distinct phase of education for children aged 3 to 5. In Great Britain this comprises Foundation and Reception. In the United States it is the equivalent of Pre-Kinder and Kinder 1. At The International Preparatory School, children in the foundation stage not only follow an academic programme, they also participate in activities throughout the school, including shows and assemblies, house activities and special events.

Language and communication

The children are given opportunities to talk and communicate in a widening range of situations, to respond to adults and to each other, to practise and extend their range of vocabulary and communication skills and to listen carefully. They learn to speak clearly and audibly with confidence and control and show their awareness of the listener by using conventions such as greetings, 'please' and 'thank you'. They learn to hear and say initial and final sounds in words and short vowel sounds within words. They link sounds to letters, naming and sounding the letters of the alphabet and begin to use their phonic knowledge to write simple words. The children have opportunities to explore, enjoy, learn about and use words and text in a broad range of contexts and to experience a rich variety of books. They become aware that print carries meaning and begin to experiment with writing by making and giving meaning to marks. They learn to use a pencil and to hold it effectively to form recognizable letters. They understand that English is read from left to right and from top to bottom. The children are encouraged to ask questions and to make patterns of their experiences through cause and effect, sequencing, ordering and grouping.

Key Stage 1

Key Stage 1 includes children from the ages of 5 to 7 and corresponds to Years 1 and 2 in the British system and Kinder II and First Grade in the United States.

The National Curriculum subjects include the following: English

In Key Stage 1 special emphasis is placed on developing the children's ability to listen carefully and respectfully when others are presenting their news or sharing with the class and when instructions and explanations are being given. The children develop their ability to speak confidently not only by expressing themselves in class but also by taking part in presentations to the whole school. Our assemblies are an important part of learning to speak before an audience. Our young students excel at this. One of our main objectives is to motivate the children to become enthusiastic readers who enjoy a variety of texts. They read stories, plays, poems, information texts and discuss the main points of these.

In writing the children develop their ability to write and communicate meaning through a variety of texts. They experiment with narrative and non-fiction writing such as poems, lists, stories, messages, etc. They use language to explore their own experiences and imaginary worlds. They are taught to use the appropriate punctuation and to reread and correct their own work. Clear, joined handwriting is developed and a variety of spelling techniques learned.

Key Stage 2

Key Stage 2 consists of Years 3 to 6 in the British system or Grades 2 to 5 in the U.S. and Chilean educational systems. In addition to a varied and stimulating curriculum, students have the opportunity to participate in many extracurricular activities. As in all stages of their education here at The International Preparatory School, assemblies and house activities continue to be important to the learning experience. The following subjects are included in the Key Stage 2 curriculum.

English

Listening and speaking skills continue to be emphasized through oral reports and sharing personal, national and international news. Performing for a wider audience takes place in the context of assemblies and participation in other school events, which contribute to developing the children's' self-confidence and speaking skills.

Reading skills are reinforced and expanded using a variety of texts, both fiction and non-fiction. Cross curricular links are made through reading and discussion of appropriate texts. The students learn to discuss characters, story development, plot, setting, etc.

They are also encouraged to read for personal growth. They explore the use of language in literary and nonliterary texts and learn how language works.

The students learn to write in a variety of contexts. While doing so they reinforce and expand the basic skills of handwriting, spelling and punctuation, their knowledge of the parts of speech and skills with reference books. Work in carried out at the word, sentence and text level with emphasis on paragraph structure and development.

Key Stage 3

Key Stage 3 consists of Years 7 to 9 in the British system (Grades 6 to 8 in the U. S. system) and is also known as Middle School. Students take the full National Curriculum span of subjects in this key stage. For more information about the key stages see **Key Stage Chart and/or Year Equivalents.**

English

In English, students develop confidence in speaking and writing for public and formal purposes. They also develop their ability to evaluate the way language is used. They read classic and contemporary texts and explore social and moral issues. In Speaking and listening students learn to speak and listen confidently in a wide variety of contexts. They learn to be flexible, adapting what they say and how they say it to different situations and people. When they speak formally or to people they do not know, they are articulate and fluent in their use of spoken standard English. They learn how to evaluate the contributions they, and others, have made to discussions and drama activities.

Key Stage 4

At Key Stage 4 students prepare to take examinations for the IGCSE (International General Certificate of Secondary Education). Students in this key stage in Great Britain are usually between 14 and 16 years old. Students who transfer to The International Preparatory School without the adequate preparation to do IGCSEs will be prepared for these examinations before proceeding on to higher level examinations such as AS (Advanced Subsidiary level) or A-levels (Advanced levels). In addition to the courses required at this level - English, Mathematics, a foreign language and science (Physics, Biology and/or Chemistry) - students may also choose History and/or Geography and Music, Art or Design and Technology.

The International Preparatory School (TIPS) is authorized by the University of Cambridge to administer examinations for the International Certificate of Secondary Education (IGCSE), AS and A-Levels, which are accepted for admission to U.K. universities as well as many other universities around the world. For more information about external examinations please go to Cambridge International Examinations.

English

In English students learn to use language confidently, both in their academic studies and for the world beyond school. They use and analyse complex features of language. They are keen readers who can read many kinds of text and make articulate and perceptive comments about them.

In Speaking and listening emphasis is placed on speaking and listening confidently in a wide variety of contexts. Students learn to be flexible, adapting what they say and how they say it to different situations and people. When they speak formally or to people they do not know, they are articulate and fluent in their use of spoken standard English. They learn how to evaluate the contributions they, and others, have made to discussions and drama activities.

Reinforcement continues for students working with English as a second or other language.

The International Preparatory School is recognized as a Centre for Cambridge International Examinations. As such, the school is authorized to administer the International Certificate of Secondary Education(IGCSE) and A-Levels, which are accepted for admission to U.K. universities as well as many universities around the world.

The International Preparatory School is regularly inspected by representatives of the U.S. State Department for its inclusion on the list of approved school for U.S. government employees and contractors. The school has also been approved for the same purposes by the British Council.

** **The International Preparatory School** is accredited by the Chilean Ministry of Education through Year 9 (Grade 8), from which point the school has elected non-inclusion.

The School Year

The school year runs from March to mid-December and is divided into two semesters. An optional summer programme is available in January. There are no classes in February. There are three weeks of winter vacation in July and one week in September for the Chilean National Holidays. For the 2012 Calendar, please click here. 2012 Calendar

Progress Reports

There are two progress reports during the year, one at the end of each semester. Parent-teacher meetings are scheduled twice a year and either parent or teacher may ask for special meetings if they feel it necessary.

The School Day

The school day begins at 9:00am and ends at 2:15 for Playgroup and Foundation students. Year 1-6 students leave school at 3:25 and those in Year 7-13 at 4:20pm. There are extracurricular activities in the afternoons from 3:35 to 5:00.

Extracurricular Activities

In addition to their regular classes, students may participate in a variety of extracurricular activities in the afternoons. These include tennis, gymnastics or cheerleading, computer lab, football (soccer), scouts, basketball, karate and music.

House Activities

The International Preparatory School has a system of "Houses" based on that used in many British schools. Our four houses are: St. Andrew, St. David, St. George and St. Patrick. The house system is intended to promote greater integration among students of all ages and cultural backgrounds, to develop the dynamics of school spirit and to encourage inter-house activities. It is also intended to develop qualities of leadership, especially among older students, who organize many activities for their houses. Each house is made up of students from different classes, from Pre-Kinder to Senior School, with a Captain and a Vice-Captain from the upper grades. As students participate in sports, cultural, social and educational activities, they earn points for their houses. Events might include Roald Dahl Day, Crazy Hat Day Famous Person Day, and Backwards Clothes Day.

Uniform

Although there is no regular school uniform, a Physical Education uniform is obligatory.

Pastor Fernandez 16001, Lo Barnechea · Santiago de Chile · Phone: (562) 321-5800 · Fax: (562) 321-5821 . info@tipschile.com

**

Model 4:

The International Baccalaureate Model (with full immersion)

Santiago College **http://bit.ly/Sb0Eoa**

Welcome Letter from the Headmistress http://bit.ly/Sb0Eoa

Thomas Jerome Baker

Thank you for taking the time to learn more about Santiago College's unique community. This site is designed for parents and guardians who are searching for a school for their children as well as current members of our community and alumni.

THE GOAL OF THIS WEBSITE IS TO PROVIDE USERS WITH CURRENT AND USEFUL INFORMATION ABOUT SANTIAGO COLLEGE. THIS IS OUR OPPORTUNITY TO SHOW YOU WHO WE ARE, WHAT WE DO AND HOW WE DO IT.

There has been something extraordinary at the heart of Santiago College since its foundation.

That *something extraordinary* explains our students' happiness and achievements, our graduates' success, and the deep bonds that our alumni maintain with Santiago College throughout their lives. We feel that this *something extraordinary* actually represents two vital forces: tradition and innovation. These two forces allow Santiago College to be a dynamic school that evolves over time even as it is sustained by an unwavering philosophy based on solid goals and values.

Few decisions in a child's life will have such far-reaching effects as the school he or she is to attend. What is at stake is nothing less than the development of the child's values and intellect, and even their career goals and active and positive participation in society. It is therefore of utmost importance that the school be compatible with the child's abilities and interests, as well as with the dreams and expectations of his/her parents or guardians. This compatibility is based on the school's philosophy of education, that is, the guiding principles and values that shape day-to-day activities. Santiago College offers its students a solid moral and intellectual foundation upon which to build their future. For over 131 years, we have used a curriculum that is active, motivating, creative, nurturing and challenging.

MILESTONES

Bilingual in Chile: An Impossible Dream?

Santiago College was one of the first schools in Chile to formally recognize that the education of women should be placed at the same level as that of men.

Santiago College was the first school in Chile to fully incorporate all three levels of the International Baccalaureate Curriculum.

Santiago College is one of the few educational institutions in Chile that has a true inter-faith curriculum, offering classes on Catholicism, Protestantism and Judaism.

HEADMISTRESS SANTIAGO COLLEGE
http://bit.ly/Sb0Eoa

Lorna Prado Scott, holds an undergraduate degree in Elementary English and Physical Education and a Master's degree in Education and Educational Management. She also holds International Baccalaureate Organization (IBO) Accreditation as a Primary Years Program (PYP) Trainer and has been a member of the PYP Curriculum and Evaluation Committee of the IBO since 2002. Over the past 20 years, Mrs. Prado has served as the Lower School and Upper School Principal. She became the Acting Headmistress of the school in 2003 and was officially appointed at the end of 2004. Mrs. Prado is a member of the Santiago College Class of 1970 and has been awarded the school's highest honor: the Finer Womanhood Award (now called the Finer Humankind Award). She has four children.

In 2007, Ms. Prado was elected by her peers to serve as one of the eight members of the Regional Heads Representative Committee (RHRC) of the International Baccalaureate Organization and on the International Heads Representative Committee (IHRC).

The **IHRC** is a group of 16 members of RHRCs (4 from each IBO region). Each RHRC has eight members elected by their peers. The role of these bodies is to advise and work with IBO on matters of concern to IB World Schools and to further the cause of international education.

SANTIAGO COLLEGE: A BILINGUAL SCHOOL

Santiago College is a bilingual Chilean school with an international curriculum. It is recognized for providing top-level English instruction. Our school combines the Chilean national curriculum with the International Baccalaureate Programs:

Primary Years Program (PYP),
Middle Years Program (MYP) and
Diploma Program.

The vast majority of Santiago College students are Chilean nationals, though we do have students from many different countries.

All **PYP** classes are taught in English except for Spanish, Religion, Physical Education (PE) and Art.

All **MYP** (Grades 6 to 8) classes are taught in English except for Religion, Physical Education (PE), Spanish, Technology and Art.

Almost all **MYP** and **Diploma Program** classes for 9th through 12th graders are taught in Spanish. However, all Santiago College graduates are expected to achieve a high level of proficiency in English.

In 2006, the school had a 100% pass rate in the IB Diploma English examinations.

Source: http://bit.ly/Sb0Eoa

**

Four models of bilingual education (English & Spanish) is what we have looked at. We have taken this look because these are the programs that are enjoying tremendous success teaching English, in Chile.

Let's be clear, these are the four most common models of

bilingual education that the highest performing schools in Chile use to ensure their students become bilingual. Yet is this all there is to it? Socioeconomic status, tertiary-educated parents, travel, future aspirations, and learning outside the classroom are also a huge part of the equation.

Let's also not forget resources like appropriate textbooks, multimedia labs, bilingual teachers, small classrooms, individualised attention, and a stable home environment. All of these factors contribute to the success of the students. as if this weren't enough, there's even more: the peer effect.

The Peer Effect

It's the effect of being in a classroom with students who are highly capable, and who share the same intellectual characteristics, a positive attitude towards learning, and highly independent learners. Being in a classroom with these kinds of peers who can mutually help one another learn, explain things, participate equally in projects and activities, - all of this - has value in making a child not only bilingual, but highly capable as a learner.

Did I miss anything? What about the myths? There are various myths about bilinguals that aren't true. You might be shocked to know that starting early is a very good idea. Learning English as a child will not harm a child's development of literacy skills in the first language. So, waiting until fifth grade to begin studying a language is not necessary.

I know. That sounds like heresy. Won't the child have trouble learning how to read Spanish if they spend their first 6 years at school learning everything in English? The answer is "No". The child will learn Spanish. Research does not support the idea that it is necessary to learn Spanish before you learn English. The Chilean experience with bilingual education is evidence of how two languages can be learned at the same time, to a high degree of competency in both languages.

And there are other myths, some of which seem to be intuitively correct, yet don't stand up to the burden of proof. I will share a few of the myths with you below. The lens we will use will be the lens of personal experience.

I have had the chance to live and work for extended periods of time in at least three countries, the United States, Germany and Chile, and as a teacher of English, it has allowed me to learn a lot about how languages are learned.

I have found that people in these countries all share the same beliefs, concepts, and interpretations about people like me, multilingual, trilingual, bilingual. I'm bilingual in English-German, English-Spanish, and trilingual in English-Spanish-German.

I reached a high level of proficiency in German by exposure and being totally immersed in German culture and life. As a student of nursing, all of my courses were taught in German. I never heard an English word for the various medical and nursing related subjects I was studying.

I experienced a silent period. I went through frustration and feelings of being overwhelmed. I wanted to give up. I felt like I'd made a mistake studying nursing in Germany, in German. On many days I just wanted to give up.

I would have given up if I had not been highly motivated and highly determined to succeed. So every day, I came back for more. It was slow, and painful, but in the end, I was able to reach a level of proficiency that was extremely high. My German was so good that I was able to graduate from nursing school and obtain a job working as a nurse on a Medical-Surgical floor in the hospital where I was trained at, where I'd been an "**Azubi**" or "**auszubildende**", a student learner.

Yes, I am aware of the misconceptions about bilingualism and bilinguals. They are a part of my personal life story, my biography. People generally believe that their attitudes and beliefs about bilingualism are logically sound. It's the same in the USA, in Germany, and in Chile.

For example, here in Chile, most people you meet don't speak English, or any other language either, well enough to be considered bilingual. Therefore, it seems quite logical to assume that true bilingualism is a rare phenomenon.

This assumption is wrong, however. In fact, it has been estimated that more than half of the world's population is bilingual. Put another way, more than 50% of all the people in the world today, uses two or more languages in everyday life. Bilingualism is found in all parts of the world, at all levels of society, in all age groups.

Really, I'm not making this up. There's the guy called Bill, 65 years old, who sells post cards in a market in Vietnam. Obviously Bill is a very poor guy. Yet he speaks English, and he's quite famous, at least by YouTube standards. Meet "Bill" (the hero on the mountain) from Saigon, Vietnam: http://bit.ly/QT71xP

Another common misconception is that bilinguals have equal knowledge of their languages. In my case, over the course of 12 years, from 1982 to 1994, I went from being monolingual in English to becoming a balanced bilingual and finally on to a dominant speaker of German.

I hadn't lost my English and become a monolingual German speaker. I simply used German every day about 99.9% of the time. I lived my life through the mediation of the German language. Along the way I discovered that I knew how to say some things in German that I did not know how to say in English. To sum up, most bilinguals are like me. We know our languages to the level of proficiency that is necessary and the language we use most often becomes the dominant one.

There are also the myths that real bilinguals do not have an accent in their different languages and that they are excellent all-around translators. For example, just last week I was asked how long I'd been in Chile. When I answered, "ten years" the other person looked at me funny and then asked me when I was going to learn the language. I can tell you that reading and writing Spanish, the passive skills, are stronger for me than my pronunciation. I've even written a book in Spanish, in addition to several articles on my blog in Spanish.

So bilingualism is not about the accent. Some of us retain our native pronunciation as we map our phonology onto the second or third language. Bilinguals do indeed have accents, especially, if they are like me, learning the second language as an adult. Having an accent or not does not make me more or less bilingual, and bilinguals often have difficulties translating specialized language.

Then there is the misconception that all bilinguals are bicultural, or in my case, tricultural. Haven't people ever heard about the cultural bias that permits foreigners to get away with cultural blunders that a native speaker would be held accountable for? I've heard it called "The Bonus", "the Gringo Effect", the "My House is Your House Effect", among others. The point I'd like to make is that we forgive people for a "faux pas", whether cultural or linguistic, if we think they are too innocent and simply unaware of a cultural norm or an appropriate linguistic use of language.

Have you heard the myth about bilinguals having split personality? According to the myth, a bilingual is supposed to be one person in one language and another, different person in the second language. Nothing could be further from the truth. It would be tiring having to slip into the character that fit each persona according to the language you are speaking.

As far as children are concerned, many worries and misconceptions are also widespread. The first is that bilingualism will delay language acquisition in young children. This was a popular myth in the first part of the last century, but there is no conclusive research evidence that supports this myth.

Their rate of language acquisition is the same as that of their monolingual counterparts. I've already shared the evidence from prominent researchers in the USA and from Canada that refute this misconception about children. Yet even today, many parents would probably not consent to placing their child in a full-immersion program in which everything was learned in English for 6 years, before then changing over to Spanish as the language of instruction in the 7th year of studies.

There is also the fear that children raised as bilinguals will always mix their languages. By the way, this is called code-switching. Did you know that the singer Shakira mixes her language in her songs? A graduate student in the linguistics program at the University of Sydney, Christian Guzman, has thoroughly researched this aspect of Shakira's songs. http://bit.ly/ScD4rr The video is highly recommended viewing. Shakira code switches in order to achieve a desired effect on the listener though. Trust me, she's not code-switching because she is unable to focus on only one language.

She's adapting her speech and her language to her audience. In fact, both monolinguals and bilinguals adapt to the situation they are in. The bilingual simply has a greater variety of pragmatic and linguistic discourse management tools at their disposal. Watch the video and draw your own conclusions about Shakira.

As for myself, when I interact in monolingual situations (e.g. with my mother-in-law (native Spanish speaker), who doesn't speak a word of English (my first language), I am monolingually Spanish. When I'm with my wife Gaby, another bilingual, we often have conversations in which she speaks Spanish to me and I respond to her in English. We are the royal couple (King and Queen) of code-switchers when we are together.

Finally, there is the worry that bilingualism will affect negatively the cognitive development of bilingual children. This book began by presenting the recent research which shows the contrary; bilingual children do better than monolingual children in certain cognitive tasks. Do you remember the executive control function?

Aside from these common misunderstandings, certain attitudes are specific to countries and areas of the world. In Europe, and also here in Chile, for example, bilingualism is seen favorably but people have very high standards for who should be considered bilingual. Perfect knowledge of their languages is expected. You are not allowed to have an accent in them, and even, in some countries, have grown up with their two (or more) languages. At that rate, very few people consider themselves bilingual even though, in Switzerland for example, the majority of the inhabitants know and use two or more languages in their everyday life.

USA

How about the United States? Einar Haugen, a pioneer of

bilingualism studies, has stated that the US has probably been the home of more bilingual speakers than any other country in the world. Bilingualism here is very diverse, pairing English with Native American languages, older colonial languages, recent immigration languages, and so on.

This said, it is not very extensive at any one time. Currently, only 17% of the population is bilingual as compared to much higher percentages in many other countries of the world. Canada, in contrast, is almost 18% bilingual.

We looked at Canada already. But what explains this low number for the USA? This is not due to the fact that new immigrants are not learning English. The reason, rather, is that bilingualism is basically short-lived and transitional in this country. For generations and generations of Americans, bilingualism has covered a brief period, spanning one or two generations, between monolingualism in a minority language and monolingualism in English.

The tolerance that America has generally shown towards minority languages over the centuries has favored the linguistic integration of its speakers. As sociologist Nathan Glazer writes, the language of minorities "shriveled in the air of freedom while they had apparently flourished under adversity in Europe".

When President Barack Obama stated that children should speak more than one language, he was probably referring to the paradox one finds in this country: on the one hand, the world's languages brought to the United States are not maintained, and they wither away, and on the other hand only a few of them are taught in schools, to too few students, and for too short a time. A national resource – the country's knowledge of the languages of the world – is being put aside and is not being maintained.

It is important to stop equating bilingualism with not knowing English and being un-American. Bilingualism means knowing and using at least two or more languages, one of which is English in the United States. Bilingualism allows you to communicate with different people and hence to discover different cultures, thereby giving you a different perspective on the world. It increases your job opportunities and it is an asset in trade and commerce. It also allows you to be an intermediary between people who do not share the same languages.

Passport to other cultures

Bilingualism is a personal enrichment and a passport to other cultures. At the very least, and to return to Barack Obama's comment, it certainly allows you to say more than "merci beaucoup" when interacting with someone of another language. One never regrets knowing several languages but one can certainly regret not knowing enough.

***

Source: **François Grosjean**, the author of ***Bilingual: Life and Reality***, received his degrees up to the Doctorat d'Etat from the University of Paris, France. He started his academic career at the University of Paris and then left for the United-States in 1974 where he taught and did research in psycholinguistics at Northeastern University, Boston.

While at Northeastern he was also a Research Affiliate at the Speech Communication Laboratory at MIT.

In 1987, he was appointed professor at Neuchâtel University, Switzerland, where he founded the Language and Speech Processing Laboratory.

He has lectured occasionally at the Universities of Basel, Zurich and Oxford. In 1998, he cofounded *Bilingualism: Language and Cognition* (Cambridge University Press).

Visit his website at: www.francoisgrosjean.ch and his Psychology Today blog, "Life as a bilingual", at:

www.psychologytoday.com/blog/life-bilingual .

http://bit.ly/gV041P

**

CHAPTER 7

A NEW GENERATION OF TEACHERS

"Education is an act of love, and this is an act of courage. You can not be afraid of the debate. You cannot evade the discussion... How do you learn to discuss and debate with an education which imposes?' ~ Paulo Freire, "*Education, as the Practice of Freedom*".

How long does it take to create a new generation of teachers who have achieved a high level of proficiency in English? I ask the question as a reflection, and thus a rhetorical question (I wonder…). Rhetorically, the question is one which does not seek an answer.

It is based on information found in the publication, "English Next", written by David Graddol.

Success or failure in the area of teaching English as a foreign language, however, may indeed hinge upon the proficiency of the teacher. Though there are many other aspects to consider, the teacher undoubtedly plays a major role.

Teaching English should not be oversimplified. Teaching English as a Foreign Language, or as a Global Language, is very complex. Still, there are three (3) aspects which seem to mark the Chilean experience more profoundly than other factors seem to do.

First, the global trend to **teach English at a very young age**, often in kindergarden, has begun to show positive results. In Chile, for example, most of the top performing schools in the 2010 SIMCE test begin teaching English in kindergarden. Starting early evidently works well for those who are willing (and able) to put the resources in place (time, materials, facilities, teachers, etc.)

Second, those teachers who are able to **teach the entire class in English** enjoy a consistently higher level of success than those teachers who are unable to teach the entire class in English. **Teaching English in English** is an aspect that is shared by those teachers who are successful.

A third consideration must be included. The most successful schools in Chile have **reduced the class size** from 45 students to numbers that range **from 20 to 25 students**. Finding some way to replicate these three aspects appears to be a "must" in the Chilean context.

I do not pretend to have an answer as to where you get the financial resources and the human resources to reduce class size. All I know is that the actual experience of our most successful schools in Chile is "telling us" to do three things:

1. Start teaching English early, preferably in kindergarden,
2. Teachers teach the entire class in English, and somehow
3. Reduce class size (20 – 25 students)

Now, let's turn to David Graddol's book, English Next, written in 2006, in which he accurately predicted the current state of affairs in EFL in Chile, as we shall see later.

Excerpt from "English Next" by David Graddol
Source:http://www.britishcouncil.org/learning-research-english-next.pdf

Why global English may mean the end of 'English as a Foreign Language

"Implementing a project which will mainly benefit future

generations is often extremely difficult for democratic governments who are re-elected every 3–5 years.

If a country decides to make English their second language, the reality is that – if they do everything right and have no untoward setbacks – they are embarking on a project which will take **30–50 years to fully mature**.

This is the length of time it took the countries which provide the main models, such as Finland (30 – 50 years).

It is, of course, true that innovation is often faster for later adopters, but many of the problems facing any country wishing to make its population bilingual in a new language are largely not ameliorated by benefiting from the experience of others or technology transfer.

One fundamental dimension is **how long it takes to create a new generation of teachers who are proficient in English**. By the time such resources are put in place, of course, **the world for which governments are preparing their populations will have moved on**.

Language education requires a **commitment and consistency** which is unusual in other policy areas. It also needs an approach which is **highly flexible and responsive to a fast-changing world**. The two are difficult to reconcile.

CATERING FOR DIVERSITY

Although there are many reasons – social, economic and practical – why **partial implementation** may be a bad idea, **in practice it seems impossible to avoid**. It seems impossible to roll out a uniform programme in all schools simultaneously.

One reason is that the **essential resources** are simply **not available**, especially a supply of **teachers who have sufficient proficiency in English**.

Countries which have attempted to recruit large numbers of native-speaker teachers have discovered that it is **impossible to attract the numbers required, with the teaching skills and experience needed, at a cost which is bearable**.

This typically leads to a multi-speed approach, where different kinds of school, and different localities, start teaching English at different ages.

But where there is extensive migration to cities, how can continuity be provided for children who move schools? Further, textbooks suitable for 12-year-old beginners are not suitable for 7-year-old early readers. During a transitional period, there will be annual changes in the age-level-content mix which textbooks need to provide.

MOPPING UP THE MESSINESS

In the early stages of implementation, it seems **inevitable that middle-class, urban areas will be most successful. Private sector** institutions will play a key role in supporting weaker students. And the cities are more likely to provide **English in the environment**, offering greater motivation and support for learning English.

But the truth may be that such messiness is **not just a transitional matter** which will eventually go away. The need to cater for diverse combinations of levels, ages, and needs **may be an enduring feature** of postmodern education.

**

Why does English matter so much?

"English is widely regarded as a **gateway to wealth** for national economies, organisations, and individuals. If that is correct, the **distribution of poverty** in future will be **closely linked** to the **distributions of English**." – David Graddol

Source: English Next by David Graddol, published by the British Council (2006)

**

English Next (India) – Interview with David Graddol

"English has become the **language of opportunity** for India."

**

The Worldwide Accent Project

This project is a collection of accents from around the world. If you'd like to take part, please do so! Just don't forget to add your video as a video response, and if you can, get your friends/parents etc to take part too!

There are NO rules for this thing, anyone can take part. If you feel that your accent doesn't fit into a particular category, don't worry, simply say how you think your accent might have been influenced.

Also, please still take part even if someone else has submitted one for your region already; the more the merrier! This video will be updated when the project has finished – so if you're reading this it's still on!

The passage:

See above those clouds, near where the blue sky appears to fold? Some say it is the entrance to the floating isles where pirates still rule the air and dragons choose to live. Only the most skilled pilots can sail their craft close enough to even glimpse the light coming from within. You can't find those who know the way; they find you. Rather, you four lazy tourists must learn from your books and be ready, so that you may not miss an opportunity to travel to that mysterious place. It would be an adventure that you would never forget. Now, I think that's enough with this pleasurable story telling. Go home and join your aunt – she's cooking fine food!

How to name your video and what to put into the description:

After you've made your video, name it "Worldwide Accent Project – [your accent location]" (for example, I would name mine "Worldwide Accent Project – Keswick, Cumbria, England", and include the following text in the description.... "This is my contribution to the Worldwide Accent Project, which is a collaboration project made by YouTubers from around the world,

with the intention of creating a global accent archive. Anybody can participate, even if English is not your first language.
http://bit.ly/U9rk94

Facebook Group: http://on.fb.me/Q1d4mZ

**

Chinglish, Singlish & Spanglish: Standard English Disappearing

Language change is inevitable. Teens and technology are a driving force behind language change today.

We know that languages change. There are countless ways to show that change. We know this to be true, languages change. Nobody finds the statement that "languages change" to be worthy of a dispute nowadays.

It's a fact, languages change. It's usually not a problem, unless you are concerned with **language purity**. For instance, there are those who believe language should be kept pure, in a standardized form, with approved words, meanings, uses, pronunciation, etc. Language change matters a lot to such people.

However, the larger question is why you and I (everyday people) should care about language change. "**So what?**", is the most important question we can ask ourselves. I mean, if I can understand you, and you can understand me, there is no problem. Any time you are using words in a way that confuses me, then I can clear up the misunderstanding by simply asking, "What do you mean by that?"

My point is that if languages change, I don't have to worry so much about change per se, but about my ability to use language in a way that is appropriate to the communicative purpose and situation I find myself in. In short, **negotiation of meaning** is the tool I use to understand you.

Another option, besides negotiation of meaning, is **being up to date on all language change**. Of course, this is nearly impossible, that is, unless you are in contact with teens.

Teens have always been willing (and able) to coin new terms, words, and phrases that suit their world view, their teen culture, and their own experience of making sense of the world.

Spanglish, Singlish, and Chinglish (non-standard forms of English), will most likely all have teens as a source of inspiration. Teens (and technology) have given us alternative ways of expression, time and time again, that in the end, have enriched our use of language overall. As a result of teens willingness to innovate with language, the **disappearance of Standard English** is on the horizon. Not!

No, it is very premature on my part to predict the demise of Standard English. For example, try speaking Chinglish, Singlish or Spanglish at a job interview for an international company. You would most likely not get the job.

Spoken English, in other words, is standardised in formal situations. We have come to expect adherence to the norms of linguistic behaviour, in formal communicative situations, from a competent language user. Again, using a non-standard form of English in a formal communicative situation is not likely to be a successful strategy.

Another example is written English, which I have used for this post. Had I written in Chinglish, Singlish or in Spanglish, I would have been at times incoherent for some of the readers. Yet is using Spanglish a strategy that always has negative communicative consequences in formal situations?

I am a bit of a maverick, and **I have written a book in Spanglish** called, "Soy Un Maestro: I Am A Teacher." It is a book that celebrates the joys and challenges of being a teacher.

Yes, it is written in Spanglish, but don't let that put you off. Take my word for it, it's one of the best books I've written about being a teacher and the teaching profession in general. Take a look for yourself, it's only $2.99:

Soy Un Maestro: I Am A Teacher [Paperback]

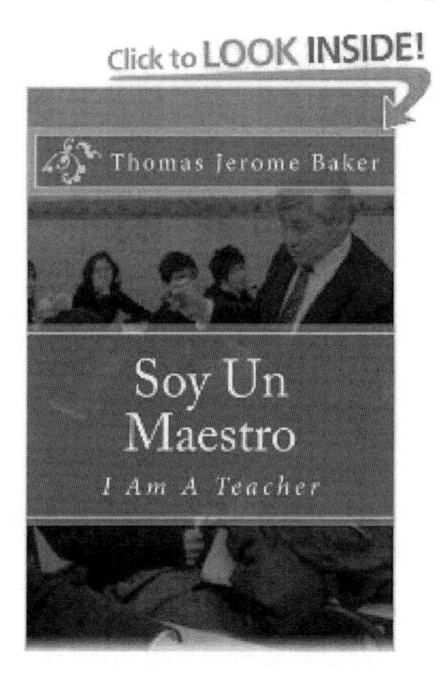

I am a teacher, and I teach in Chile. This year a new Teacher Career Law, defining the teaching profession in terms of increased prestige, attracting more applicants from higher performing students, an obligatory enabling exam, higher salaries, fewer hours teaching in the classroom, and higher responsibilities will be passed, hopefully. This book totally supports the idea that a good law is needed, and now is the time to pass one, even if that law is not yet perfect.

We teachers have such a long way to go, and this is clearly a tremendous step in the right direction. To celebrate, all of the funds received for the sale of this book will go to support the EdCamp Santiago free conference for teachers in Chile. Thank you, in advance, for buying this book. May God Bless You…

Soy el más afortunado de todos quienes trabajan. A un médico se le permite traer una vida en un momento mágico. A mí se me permite que esa vida renazca día a a día con nuevas preguntas, ideas y amistades. Un arquitecto sabe que si construye con cuidado, su estructura puede permanecer por siglos. Un maestro sabe que si construye con amor y verdad, lo que construya durará para siempre.

Book Details
Paperback: **170 pages**
Publisher: CreateSpace (July 3, 2012)
Language: English/Spanish
ISBN-10: 1478176520
ISBN-13: 978-1478176527

Soy Un Maestro: I Am A Teacher [Kindle Edition]

Soy Un Maestro: I Am A Teacher [Kindle Edition]

CHAPTER 8

BILINGUAL SINGAPORE

Speech by Mr Lee Kuan Yew, Former Minister Mentor and current Senior Advisor to Government of Singapore Investment Corporation at the Launch of the English Language Institute of Singapore (ELIS) on Tuesday, 6 September 2011, at the Marina Bay Sands Expo and Convention Centre.

Minister for Education
Mr Heng Swee Keat
Principals and teachers
Ladies and gentlemen

It gives me great pleasure to be present this afternoon at the launch of the English Language Institute of Singapore or ELIS for short. The launch of ELIS shows how far Singapore has come in terms of establishing English as the lingua franca among what was, 46 years ago, a community of polyglots, speaking a variety of dialects and languages.

Historical Importance of English

When Singapore became independent in 1965, we had a population that spoke a range of different dialects and languages. This was a result of the colonial education system which favoured the English-speaking, but allowed vernacular schools with different mediums of instruction to co-exist.

Political and economic realities led us to choose English as our working language. 75% of the population then was Chinese, speaking a range of dialects; 14% Malays; and 8% Indians. Making Chinese the official language of Singapore was out of the question as the 25% who were non-Chinese would revolt.

In addition, the geographical reality was, and remains today, that Singapore would be economically isolated from the wider world if Chinese was chosen. And China then could not be of much help to our economic development. With barely 700 sq km of land, we could not make a living out of agriculture.

Trade and industry was our only hope for economic survival.

To attract investors here to set up their manufacturing plants, our people had to speak English, the language that is either the first or second language of the major economies of the world.

English was our best choice, the language of international diplomacy, science and technology, and international finance and commerce after World War II.

The British had spread the English language across several hundred millions in Asia, especially India and Africa, besides the old Commonwealth of Canada, South Africa, Australia and New Zealand.

The Americans inherited this huge English speaking mass when they became the dominant power after World War II and made it the largest language spoken across many nations. The choice of English as our lingua franca gave all races equal opportunities through a common language to learn, communicate and work in.

We kept our original languages by our policy of bilingualism, allowing opportunities for people to study their respective mother tongues. This built a sense of belonging to their original roots and increased their self-confidence and self-respect. Thus, a united multi-ethnic, multi-lingual people ensured Singapore's survival. Had we not chosen English, we would have been left behind.

Current Importance of English

We are the only country in the region that uses English as our working language, the main medium of instruction in our schools. This has given our young a strong advantage of growing up in a multi-cultural, multi-lingual society, all speaking the international language of commerce and trade, English, and their mother tongues, Chinese, Malay, Tamil, and others as their second languages.

English-speaking Singaporeans are sought after by MNCs, international organisations and NGOs because we can connect with the English-speaking world, and can operate comfortably in multi-cultural environments, in countries like China, India, Malaysia and Indonesia.

Singaporeans add value to these economies by being able to speak both English and Mandarin and other major Asian languages, acting as a bridge between them and the peoples of America, Europe, Japan, India and ASEAN countries.

As an English-speaking society, we have drawn foreign talent to our shores. There is an intense worldwide competition for talent, especially for English-speaking skilled professionals, managers and executives. Our English-speaking environment is one reason why Singapore has managed to attract a number of these talented individuals to complement our own talent pool.

They find it easy to work and live in Singapore, and remain plugged into the global economy. Singapore is a popular educational choice for many young Asians who want to learn English, and they get a quality education. This has kept our city vibrant.

Future Challenges

English has given Singapore a head start vis-à-vis our neighbours; but this competitive edge is not permanent. Today, because competence in English is no longer just a competitive advantage, many countries are trying to teach their children English.

It is a basic skill that many children want to acquire in the 21st century. Many countries in the region realise the importance of schooling their young in English. But it will take decades to restructure a country's language policy.

For example, the demand for English teachers in these countries has grown in recent years and English schools are mushrooming in China, Thailand and Vietnam. This is a worldwide phenomenon.

Even native English speaking countries are concerned about the standard of English among their people. The UK and the US want to raise their standards of English.

Importance of Effective Communication in the 21st Century

How do young Singaporeans fare in this increasingly competitive landscape? How well do our young people communicate, and how can we ensure that they are able to hold their own in the future?

Communication skills are one of the most important competencies needed in the 21st century workforce. If one is to succeed, he or she will need a mastery of English because it is the language of business, science, diplomacy and academia.

We have built a good English language foundation for our students. Our achievements in international benchmark tests like Programme for International Student Assessment (PISA)1 and Progress in International Reading Study (PIRLS)2 are well documented.

We can do better.

We must help every child to attain higher standards in English, and our best students must be able to hold their own internationally. Home background plays an important role in developing good English language skills.

And we are maintaining our mother tongues.

This makes it difficult unless children are exposed to the two languages early in life, from the time they are babies, according to research by specialists including Dr Jeanette Vos. However, not all our homes have this practice. We must ensure that all children, regardless of their backgrounds, have equal access to a quality education in our schools.

To maintain the high standards of English competency in Singapore, we need to ensure that from the time a child steps into kindergarten, he is exposed to good English.

Our schools must provide a rich language environment.

There must be a strong reading culture where children can access and enjoy good books.

There must be a culture of oracy.

Opportunities must be given to students to speak in English.

Students must present information and ideas, to clarify and to debate robustly with each other in English.

Developing a high level of English language competency in our students cannot be the work of the English teacher alone.

It is the responsibility of every teacher who teaches subjects in English. Teachers must use good English when they question, speak and write in the classroom. They are the best role models for our children if our young are to be effective communicators.

In leading this, there is no more important person than the Principal. Principals must foster a culture where good English permeates every classroom and every interaction between teachers and students. We must galvanise the whole school community to be role models of good English. Together, we must encourage our students to speak well, read widely and constantly to improve their English competency.

Conclusion

The launch of ELIS is timely.

You, the educators, must be the standard-bearers of the language. You need to encourage, stimulate and challenge your students to be excellent communicators in English, able to hold their own at home and abroad.

You must, yourselves, constantly seek to improve your own command and appreciation of the language so that you can engender the same love and appreciation of English in your students.

Our teachers have a strong sense of mission, and a desire to prepare our young. Upgrade your skills and your competency in English, so that you can play an important role in grooming future generations. I congratulate ELIS on its launch and look forward to the Institute improving the teaching of English in our schools.

Thank you.

*Footnote

In 2009, Singapore participated for the first time in the PISA which studies the capacity of students near the end of secondary education, to apply knowledge and skills in Reading, Mathematics and Science in a variety of real-life situations.

A total of 5,152 15-year-old students from 167 secondary schools and 131 students from 4 private schools in Singapore participated in PISA. Singapore was the top performing country among those that administered the assessment in English.

Our students performed significantly better in Reading than those from traditionally English-speaking countries such as Australia (9th), the United States (17th), Ireland (21st) and the United Kingdom (25th) and were on a par with students from Canada (6th) and New Zealand (7th).

Singapore emerged 4th out of 45 education systems that participated in PIRLS 2006. The PIRLS 2006 results affirm that Singapore's approach to the teaching of English Language is progressing in the right direction.

Schools and parents should continue to work in close partnership to foster good reading habits in our pupils, including providing a home environment which encourages reading.

**

CHAPTER 9

Birth of the Native Speaker

Birth. New Life. Beginnings. The magic, mystique, and magnificence of creating something that we hope will be greater than ourselves. The Berlitz "method", the precise moment of its birth, is a story best told by Berlitz. Travel back in time with me to the year 1870. We are at the Warner Polytechnic College, in Providence, Rhode Island, USA. Let's let Berlitz tell the story, the Birth of the Berlitz Method (Native Speaker Myth):

"Maximilian Berlitz grew up in the Black Forest region of Germany, the son of a family of teachers and mathematicians. He emigrated to the United States in 1870. The language fan, Maximilian taught Greek, Latin and six other European languages there, using the strict, traditional "grammar-translation" method.

After he had successfully taught as a private tutor for a while, he joined the Warner Polytechnic College in Providence, where he became Professor of French and German. However, the college was not as impressive as its name. Berlitz was soon the owner, dean, head teacher and the only member of the faculty, all rolled into one.

As he needed an assistant for French, Berlitz employed a young Frenchman named Joly, who obviously came with top references. When Joly arrived in Providence, he found that his employer was completely exhausted, feverish and very ill. The situation only worsened when Berlitz found out that his new assistant did not speak a single word of English. Desperately trying to find a way to use Joly in his teaching, Berlitz instructed him to explain objects using gestures and to act out verbs as well as he could. He then returned to bed.

The birth of the Berlitz Method®

He returned to the classroom six weeks later, expecting his desperate students to be angry with him. Instead, he found his students engaging in an animated exchange of questions and answers – in elegant French. The normal venerable atmosphere of a traditional classroom had disappeared. His students were also much further ahead in terms of what they had learned than Berlitz would have achieved in the same period of time. Berlitz came to a significant conclusion: the "emergency solution" had formed the basis for a completely new method of teaching. The strict learning method (Grammar Translation Method) had to give way to an animated process of discovery."

*** End of Story

What an exciting story! Sadly, it is only a story, with a number of fallacies. I shall return to those fallacies in a later post. More importantly, however, is that we recognize what happened. Berlitz rationalized that the only difference between his teaching and that of the Frenchman, "Joly", was that Berlitz was a non-native speaker of French, and that Joly was a monolingual native speaker of French. Hence, a Native Speaker was superior to a Non-native Speaker.

Berlitz committed a fallacy in his reasoning called, in Latin, "Post hoc, ergo propter hoc". This means, literally, "After this, therefore caused by this". So, first you have the non-native speaker teacher (Berlitz was a native German speaker – teaching French) and poor results. Next comes the monolingual, native French teacher, Joly. Excellent results. So Berlitz concludes that the excellent results were caused by the students having a native speaker teacher.

What's wrong with the conclusion of Berlitz? Why was Berlitz not correct in his reasoning? Let's work with this a bit, shall, we?

1. Sample size: Berlitz had only a small class. The results he had were applicable only to a small, limited number of people.

2. Random selection: The students were not randomly selected, meaning that the students participating were not chosen by a lottery system, with some students attending, and some students not attending the class.

3. Control group: There was no control group, that is, a group of students who received instruction using a different method.

4. There was no comparison group, who would have received both grammar translation and "the new Berlitz method".

5. Male and Female? How many of each gender? Results for each gender?

6. Pretest? What was the starting level of French? (Before the new method, or treatment, was applied?)

7. Post-test: What were the results after the course of treatment? Better? Worse?

8. Sustainability: Test after 1 year? 2 years? 5 years?

9. Longitudinal study? 2 years, 5 years, 10 years, 20 years?

10. Age of students?

11. Level of French of the students?

12. Motivation of the students?

13. Socioeconomic status of the students?

14. Replication: Have other investigators/researchers been able to duplicate your results, using the technique/method/conditions described by Berlitz?

15. Is there a large body of corroborating evidence, from many different sources, different researchers? (After 140 years, this should be the case)

Quite simply, Berlitz arrived at his conclusion through reasoning, what to him, intuitively explained the results he was seeing. His conclusions were at best, applicable only to that small group of students taught by himself and Joly.

Let me try to explain why this is bad science:

Imagine that Berlitz's students found him stressed out, tired, over-worked, strict, boring, and uninspiring. It's winter, it's freezing cold, and here's Berlitz drilling them on translating the classics. Berlitz gets sick, and here comes this Frenchman, Joly, speaking only French, talking about Paris, the Eiffel Tower, French cuisine, Notre Dame, Montmartre, Moulin Rouge, Mona Lisa, the Louvre, etc.

Let me give you another story: Imagine that Berlitz's students had not had any fruit, for example, oranges, to eat. Suddenly, oranges are available, and the students' results improve. Berlitz would conclude that the oranges caused the improved results.

In both examples I have given you, there is something at work called the "Unknown Variable". Basically, it means that the results are being caused by some unknown variable, and not the reason or factor that you think is responsible for the improved results.

To conclude, Berlitz was not very rigorous in his conclusion about the Native Speaker. Yet he developed a method, based on his observations of the results a Native Speaker, Joly, that have changed little from 1870 to the present date – 2010. In other words, the Myth of the Native Speaker as the superior teacher dates back 140 years.

Berlitz, as we know it today, continues to employ the method, based on the Native Speaker Myth. World-wide, any advertisement for employment as a teacher at any of the more than 500 Berlitz Centers will include this qualification line:

Qualification Requirements:

Native English speaker

And we have come back to the beginning, the Native Speaker Myth. Next, we shall discuss immigration, and how monolingual teachers of immigrants had no choice but to use English only in the classroom, with their multi-lingual classes. But that's another story…

Thomas Baker
Native Speaker
Teacher of English
Santiago, Chile

CHAPTER 10

ENGLISH ONLY

According to the American Civil Liberties Union (ACLU), the USA was a country very rich in language diversity up until the 1800s. Tolerance was the word of the day. But in 1911 something drastic happened. The Federal Immigration Commission falsely reported that while the "old Scandinavian and German immigrants" had quickly assimilated, the "new Italian and Eastern European immigrants" were inferior, less willing to learn English, and more prone to political subversion.

In order to Americanize the immigrants and exclude people thought to be of the lower classes (undesirable), English literacy requirements were established for public employment, naturalization, immigration and voting.

One million Yiddish-speaking citizens **lost their right to vote** when New York amended its voting laws to **require English**.

In California, the same thing happened to the Chinese.

Native American Indian children were taken from their families and placed in boarding schools, where they were **punished** for **speaking their native language**.

The goal was to Americanize the children…

And then along comes World War I with Germany…

In 1918, Ex-President Theodore Roosevelt famously said, "English should be the only language taught or used in the public schools. We have room for but one language in this country, and that is the English language".

In 1918, the state of Iowa outlawed the use of all foreign languages in schools.

Texas went one step further. In 1918, Texas made teaching in Spanish a crime.

In 1919, the state of Nebraska passed a law prohibiting the use of any other language than English through the eighth grade (8th).

In 1921, "English Only" education was approved for all public schools in Louisiana.

Dear reader, do you notice a trend here? Is a pattern beginning to develop?

This isn't rocket science. The Berlitz "Native Speaker Myth" had found a perfect ally in the political climate regarding language instruction only in English. "English Only" and the Myth of the Native Speaker as the best teacher, had a perfect marriage, each one benefitting from the other.

During this time period, from 1900 to 1921, a teacher of English, monolingual, with a multilingual class, would have felt it was his civic and patriotic duty to enforce an English only policy in the classroom.

Here are some quotes taken from textbooks of the era:

1904 – Harrington and Cunningham, in "First Book for Non-English-Speaking People": "English is learned by using it in the classroom".

1909 – Sara R. O'Brien, in "English for Foreigners": "English should always be the language of the classroom".

1919 – Dr. Henry H. Goldberger, in "Teaching English to the Foreign Born": "…teach English by using English as the means of instruction".

1919 – John Almack, in "Americanization: A Suggested Outline For Teachers of Aliens": "The psychological moment is at hand to make our mother tongue (English) the universal language."

Finally, let's point out that it would have been impossible to be fluent in all the languages of the immigrants. The mindset was, "these immigrants have to understand me, and try to talk like me, if they want to have any chance of improving themselves economically, socially, and culturally".

To conclude, there can be no doubt that the Native Speaker Myth was by now deeply entrenched as an ideological principle. It seemed unlikely that the Myth would keep growing any deeper in the minds of the world.

Incredibly, the Myth continued to grow even deeper, thanks to the 1961 Makerere Conference and a linguist named Noam Chomsky. This will be the subject of another book, due to its profound implications for the teaching and learning of English during the rest of the century, and indeed, even up to the present date.

See you tomorrow with another piece of the puzzle, why we have come to accept the Native Speaker Myth so thoroughly…

Thomas Baker
Native Speaker
Teacher of English as a Foreign Language
Santiago, Chile

ABOUT THE AUTHOR

Thomas Jerome Baker is the Past President of TESOL Chile (2010–2011). He is the Co-founder and Co-Organiser of EdCamp Santiago. Thomas is a member of the “Comunidad de Innovación Escolar” (Education Innovation Community) of the Telefónica Foundation and the Education 2020 Foundation.

Thomas is also a past member (2011-2012) of the International Higher Education Teaching and Learning Association, where he also serves as a reviewer and as the HETL Ambassador for Chile.

Thomas enjoys writing about a wide variety of topics. Thus far he has written the folowing genres: romance, historical fiction, autobiographical, sports history/biography, and English Language Teaching, including contemporary education in Chile. He has self-published 65 books, all of which are available on Amazon.

The source and inspiration for his writing comes from his family, his wife Gabriela, and his son, Thomas Jerome Baker, Jr.

http://www.amazon.com/Thomas-Jerome-Baker/e/B007G9HJFM

Printed in Poland
by Amazon Fulfillment
Poland Sp. z o.o., Wrocław